ISBN: 978-1-59571-832-7

Library of Congress Control Number: 2012921516

Designed and published by

Word Association Publishers
205 Fifth Avenue
Tarentum, Pennsylvania 15084

www.wordassociation.com
1.800.827.7903

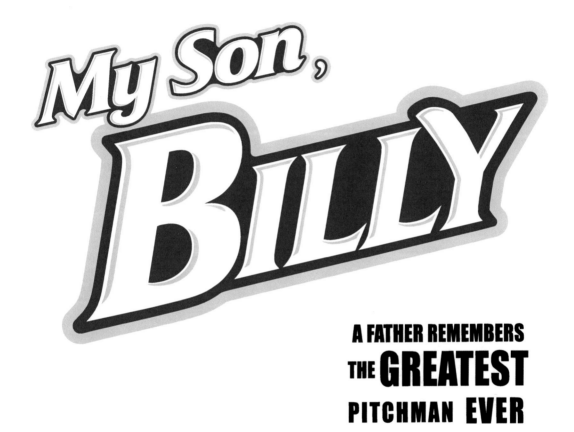

My Son, BILLY

A FATHER REMEMBERS
THE GREATEST
PITCHMAN EVER

BILL MAYS, SR

with MARC E. VIROSTEK

This book is dedicated to:
Little Billy & Elizabeth

A letter to my son Billy,

I am now putting the finishing touches on this book that's taken me two years to complete. June 28, 2010. It's been quite a while now since that fateful phone call I'll never forget until I take my last breath. It's taken me this long to finally put my thoughts into written words. Today would've been your 53rd birthday, Son! This is my birthday present to you, Billy. Writing this book has been a catharsis for me. I have done my best to find answers to my questions. I have dug deep and have spent countless hours searching and researching. I was able to uncover a lot. Some things are better left unsaid. I'm sure we'll have much to talk about when we meet again.

I love you.
—Dad

Randy, Gary, Billy, and Dee.

My Brother Billy

Billy Mays was more than a brother; he was my mentor and my idol. There isn't a day that goes by that I don't miss him or think about him in some way. He was liked by so many people in life because that is just the kind of person he was. He was the kindest person I have ever known, and I am very honored to be his brother.

—Gary Mays

For the countless fans of my brother Billy, *My Son, Billy* is a must read. Fast moving and entertaining, the author (my father) takes an arduous, sometimes painful, look at the life of America's favorite pitchman. Dad, Billy is most definitely looking down with a smile as you have "set the record straight." From his childhood to his passing, you take his fans inside the private life of, as some have called him, a television icon. I never saw him in that light (as an icon) because he remained humble and grateful until the very end. Blessed with the gift of giving, his deepest desire was to give back… to his family, his friends, and his community. Thank you for seeing this project through! I know it wasn't easy.

"Hi, Billy Mays here" not physically… but still here.

—Randy Mays

CONTENTS

Chapter 1
A Dream

I had a dream about Billy almost one year to the day after his death. Billy was sitting on the floor, dressed casually in jeans. As he got up, I noticed he was very thin and fit. He walked over to me and there was no limp – no trouble walking whatsoever. He put his hands on his hips and beamed, "Look Dad, no more pain. My hip is perfect. Those days of agony from those old football injuries are gone! And I didn't have to endure that operation. I've never felt better." He hugged me with his usual big old bear hug just like he used to! In the background, there was a little blonde girl that I thought might be his daughter, Elizabeth. It wasn't. I recognized her face but I couldn't place it. Maybe it was my Uncle Victor's girl, Louise, who drowned so long ago. There was a long couch with young children all along it. Billy loved children and he enjoyed acting goofy to entertain them. It was no surprise to me that he seemed happy and content with children all around him. In the distance, I could see sailboats on the water with full masts. Billy loved the water and I could see he was at peace here and pain free. This dream comforted me. For many nights to come when I closed my eyes I knew Billy was okay. I distinctly remember watching him fade away but before he left completely he turned around and said, "Dad! Set the record straight. Tell the truth. Do it for my children and for those I loved and left behind." All I can remember seeing as he faded away was the trademark thumbs up in the air and a big smile on his face.

I tried to figure out what he meant by all of this. In fact, I started to get depressed all over again. Then one morning I woke up with the idea of writing a book about how Billy really got started. Recently, I found out Billy had gone to NY in May, one month before his death, to talk to a publisher about a book deal. Now it was all up to me to tell his story.

Three Generations

Billy and little Billy
swimming in Florida

Having a
swim with Elizabeth

Billy with cousins
Antonio, Giovanni,
and Guiseppe

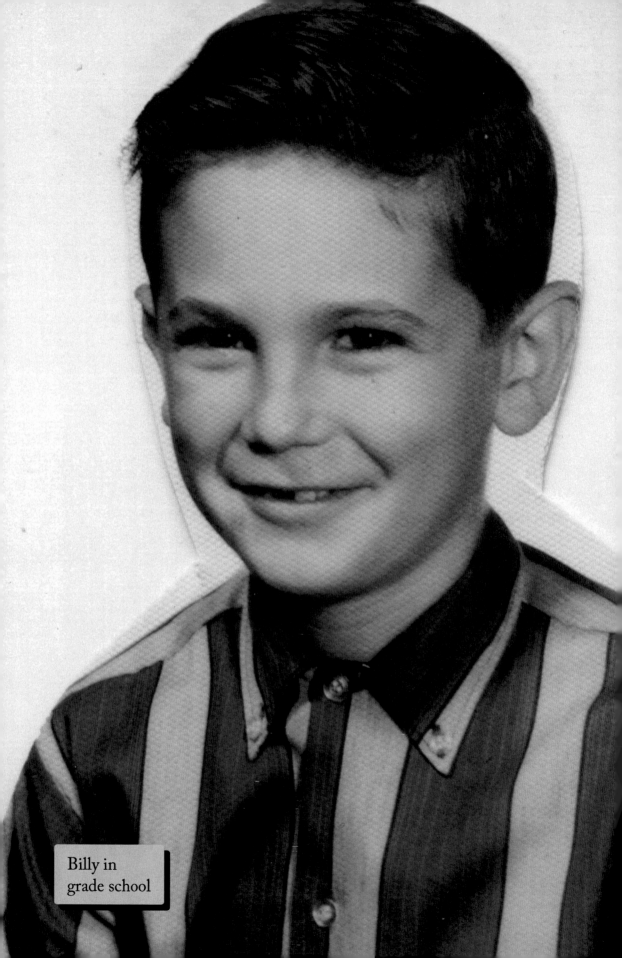

Billy in
grade school

Chapter 2
The Wrong Phone Call

I had a strange feeling the morning of June 28, 2009. It was a beautiful Saturday morning in June as I listened to the radio while coming back from breakfast. I remember checking my cell phone to make sure it was on. I was expecting a call from Billy that morning. Yep, it was on, but no call from Billy yet. Monday, Billy would be having his third hip operation, and I was concerned. Concerned because this would be the third and final attempt for Billy. The last operation, a year before, Billy's hipbone crumbled – the first operation he had a staph infection and then had a calcium build-up as a result of the second operation. And now, dear God, let this operation work. The doctors cautioned my son that this was the last operation his hip could take. If this didn't work, what then? My son told me that everything would be taken care of if something were to happen during his surgery. He specifically indicated that we were all provided for. I said, "Billy, don't talk so silly – you'll be around to see your great-grandchildren!"

As I went to dig the cell phone out of my pocket again, it fell to the floor. I pulled my truck over to the side of the road to grab it, and just as I started to pull out from the berm, a call came in. I looked at the area code and yeah, it was from Florida. My son must have slept in this morning. Why not? He had been in Philadelphia yesterday filming the Oxi Clean commercial for most of the day, and then on the way home he'd had a pretty rough flight. Billy had called me while he was stuck on US Airways flight 1241 and told me how he was hit in the head when the plane they were on made a rough landing. "It was a close call, Dad! The plane hit so hard the tires blew out. All of a sudden, as we hit, all of the things from the overhead compartments started dropping. Something hit me on the head, but I got a hard head! I just want to relax, get home, hug Elizabeth, and rest up for Monday."

I begged him to go to the hospital but he assured me he was fine, laughed, and told me, "Don't worry, Dad. This was a whirlwind trip and I'm exhausted, that's all. I have been gone for two weeks. Did you see the Conan O'Brien show? Kathy usually tapes it, so you can watch it when you get up. Conan jokingly said he hears my voice when he's going to sleep at night – yelling at him to buy something. But you wouldn't know would you, Dad? You're already in bed!" Billy always teased me about my crazy sleep schedule, because I go to bed around 7 p.m. and get up between 3 and 4 a.m. "Sorry I haven't called for a few days, but it's been nonstop. I'll call you tomorrow when I get up. Love you, Dad!"

As I sat there in my truck and answered the phone I thought, "I hope Billy is ready for Monday." My former wife Joyce was all packed and leaving that day to go down to Florida to be with him. "Billy? Billy?" It was my daughter-in-law Deborah instead. I could barely make out what she was saying. All I could hear was Deborah crying, sobbing hysterically. "I can't wake him up! Billy is dead!" My heart sank, filled with shock and disbelief. This had to be someone playing a sick joke on me. It sounded like my daughter in-law but because of the crying I wasn't sure. Thank God I was finally in front of my house. My wife saw my truck and came out crying and screaming, "Billy is dead! Billy is dead!"

I made my way into the house and the TV was on. "Pitchman Billy Mays is dead. His voice is silenced forever..." I heard them announce. My son. My son Billy. How could this be? I felt my blood pressure go up and the start of the worst headache of my entire life. God, please let this be a bad dream. I sank into my chair. Dead. My son dead. How? Why? The phone was ringing, and people were coming to the house. Still no answer – how could this happen to my son? Yet another tragedy in the Mays family. I found myself asking my wife, "Any word from Deborah?" Kathy would try and comfort me and quietly answered, "No Bill. She is probably too distraught to call."

During the coming week, I was numb. Time stopped and I waited for any morsel of news from Florida. The TV and radio were off. I refused to listen to the media. Allegations arose that my son had died from cocaine use, based on the Hillsborough medical examiner's autopsy report. Family members and friends came to the house on a steady basis. I couldn't get away from the news they had to report. They constantly asked if I was O.K. and gave me bits and pieces of news about Billy.

Kathy asked if I knew about Billy ever using cocaine. My answer was curt as I defended my son. "Why would you ever think that about Billy?" I was hurt and I later apologized for my abruptness towards her. My nerves were raw and all I wanted was for all of this to go away.

Well-known Pittsburgh coroner Cyril Wecht was interviewed on Jane Valez-Mitchell's television show, saying, "The Hillsborough County medical examiner botched Billy Mays' autopsy." Billy's brother Randy also spoke with Dr. Wecht and felt he should have been asked to do another autopsy—but ultimately it was up to Deborah to make this decision. Deborah decided to have an independent evaluation done, but by Dr. William Manion instead.

Independent Evaluation Finds that Billy Mays Death Was Not Attributable to Cocaine Usage. Statement from Deborah Mays

Tampa, Fla. – (Oct. XX, 2009) – Billy's family and I have never agreed with the Hillsborough County Medical Examiner's conclusion that cocaine use contributed to Billy's death. We found this to be so upsetting that we asked for review by an independent medical examiner.

This review, conducted by Dr. William L. Manion, concludes that the autopsy results do not support the conclusion that cocaine caused Billy's death. In fact, one of the few areas of agreement between the two reports is that it was a "natural" death. Dr. Manion goes on to say that if cocaine had been considered a significant contributing factor, the manner of death would be classified as "accidental" and not "natural."

Dr. Manion's report also says:

"…Chronic cocaine use was not demonstrated by the autopsy findings of Mr. William Mays. In addition, there is nothing in his medical, social or professional history to suggest chronic cocaine use. Therefore, I do not believe cocaine played a significant contributing factor in the death of Mr. Mays as the autopsy specimens and findings are not consistent with the cardiac conditions normally observed in a person chronically using cocaine."

Dr Manion, M.D., Ph.D., J.D., is the Medical Examiner for Burlington and Ocean Counties, New Jersey and the Chief of Pathology for Virtua Health in New Jersey. He is Board Certified by the American Board of Pathology in both Anatomic and Clinical Pathology and Forensic Pathology, and is a nationally recognized and respected expert in the field of pathology.

We believed at the time – and believe even more now based on Dr. Manion's report – that the conclusions drawn by the Hillsborough County Medical Examiner were not supported by the facts of the autopsy, nor by Billy's medical history. And, although we cannot undo the damage that has already been done to Billy's reputation, we are hopeful that this information will assist in clearing the name of a good husband, father and friend.

This has been a very difficult period for our family and we appreciate the continued support that Billy's many fans have extended. We again thank those fans and the members of the media who have respected our family's privacy. We are also grateful to Dr. Manion for this thoughtful and objective review of Billy's autopsy information and the medical literature to make sense of Billy's untimely death.

Died June 28
Lena (Nuna) Mays *1992*
Billy Mays *2009*

Chapter 3
A Cold Winter Day

That Friday was a gloomy day as I stood there staring at Musmanno's funeral home. Still in disbelief and shock, I made my way into the place where my son was. My burning tears stung so bad that I threw my head into my hands. Finally, I made my way to Billy lying there. I touched him and he felt so cold. I remembered a day long ago when he was a young boy and he felt that cold.

I closed my eyes and I could see Billy at age 4, on that cold winter's day in Hookstown. Billy loved to come with me to the job sites. This particular day, I went down to Hookstown where we were stripping coal. It was bitter cold and Billy was shivering, so I took him back to my 1950 Oldsmobile. The car wouldn't start. I panicked. We were twenty-five miles away from home, and it was downright cold. The only thing to do was to start the 1952 truck, fitted on the front with a drill for depositing dynamite on the site. What a fabulous sound when that truck started. I wrapped Billy up with an old towel, and took off my coat as he said, "I'm treezin Daddy! Treezin." I held him close to my chest and waited till he finally got warm. Not much heat in that old truck, but we made it back home. Home to Phillips Lane in Robinson Township. PA. No cell phones in those days. No one to call for help, but Nunna was there with a cup of hot cocoa for Billy and a steaming cup of black coffee with a shot of Crown Royal for me.

In those days, I lived on the family farm with Mom and Dad. Right around this time, I had to admit that my marriage wasn't going to work out and I lived in my car for two weeks before I got up the nerve to tell my parents. Eventually, I moved back into my parents' home and life started becoming better. Dad passed in 1972, so he was there for Billy till then. Those days on the farm were filled with hard work, good homemade food, a Nunna, and a Pap Pap for my three boys. I had my sons every weekend, and I lived for those precious hours. I was a better father than when I was married. I knew I only had so many hours, and I filled all of them with just them. My three sons Billy, Gary, and Randy were close in age, and became each other's buddies. Billy and Gary shared the same birthday. As the psychologists now say, "quality time not quantity." At this time, I gave them both. No time for a new life for me, or finding a new wife. My life was work and my three sons. Weekends were for big family get-togethers and bonding with them. Now, I felt totally helpless looking down at my Billy and not being able to make my son warm again.

Little Billy and me playing in the snow,
and the playhouse I built

BELOVED HUSBAND
FATHER AND SON

BILLY MAYS

1958 — 2009

"PITCHMAN"

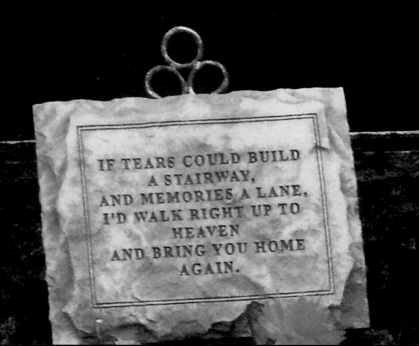

IF TEARS COULD BUILD
A STAIRWAY,
AND MEMORIES A LANE,
I'D WALK RIGHT UP TO
HEAVEN
AND BRING YOU HOME
AGAIN.

Chapter 4
Funeral

People came in droves. Over 1000 people came from all over the country. You never saw so many grown men crying like hurt children over the casket. I felt a tug at my shirtsleeve. As I turned around, I had to look down, only to see my granddaughter Elizabeth, looking at me with her soft blue eyes and golden curls. "Pap Pap, are you sad?" I was overcome with sadness as I thought of a child without her father. I fought back the tears and nodded, and she said "Me too!" How many times I would hear her say, "I miss my daddy." With that, she turned around and quickly disappeared into the back room where her cousins were on the floor playing with toys. Someone was smart enough to make sure the children were entertained during this stressful ordeal. My nephew Hal's daughter Georgia is just about the same age as Elizabeth, and they were enjoying each other's company, totally oblivious as to what was going on around them. I felt comfortable knowing where she was. As I made my way back to Billy, I watched Billy's first wife, Dee Dee, standing at the casket. She was fixated only on him, and I caught her caressing his hair lovingly and touching his hand. Billy's oldest child, now in his twenties, we still affectionately call "Little Billy," consoled his mother as she tried to compose herself. Dee Dee adored Billy and it was no secret that she was still in love with him. I always thought Billy and Dee Dee would put their differences behind them and reconcile. Even after the divorce, Dee Dee and I would get together over lunch to catch up, and I was always there to help with Little Billy. Dee Dee was family and I could wrap my arms around her and share her heartbreak. I couldn't do that with Deborah. She was very matter-of-fact and proper. Everything was on her terms – I felt like an outsider around her. Deborah spent most of her time in an adjoining room with her family.

There was a period of time when Billy was struggling with the decision to go back to Dee Dee or marry Deborah. He was conflicted and as we sat over lunch, he shared this with me. I listened and he talked. Deborah had given him an ultimatum. She threatened to relocate to Tennessee with the intention of starting a new life if Billy chose not to get married. Dee Dee was sweet and accommodating, whereas Deborah was emotionally controlling. Looking back now, I realize that was probably an idle threat; she was too connected to her family to ever move away.

Deborah was a package neatly wrapped. I often wondered if Billy wanted the opposite of what he had had. Both his mother, Joyce, and Dee Dee were both passionate, Italian women whose emotions ran deep. I feel my son was compulsive and in his quest for a mate he needed an organized woman who would share his need for "structure." Billy needed this in order to survive.

Deborah's blondish hair reminded me of the Breck ads I used to see on TV. Every hair was in place! Billy's mother was sitting alone, sobbing her eyes out while Deborah remained totally composed throughout the entire funeral. I would only hope that Deborah had her time of mourning before she came to Pittsburgh. How she was so put together amazed me, when I noticed I had on one brown sock and one black sock. Her outfit was well thought out just like her attention to details during the funeral. It made me wonder if this was the way she ran their home? It all seemed very militant to me – whenever I think back to my many visits to their home, it was run like a business. Deborah was much younger than Billy, but that wasn't his attraction to her. Her refinement was what drew him to her. She knew how to speak intelligently with colleagues. Her education was admired and respected by Billy. I often think Billy felt insecure about his lack of a good college education. I used to tell him, "Billy, you make more than any doctor or lawyer I know." He would smile and say, "But they have status and I'm not sophisticated like Deborah is." That is what he lacked and found in Deborah. When Kathy and I would visit them, we both felt uneasy even though we were treated well. It was almost like sitting at a formal table and not knowing which fork to use when.

My legs were so weak. I felt faint. The smell of all of the baskets of flowers made me nauseous. All I could do was try and compose myself, for the sake of my grandson Little Billy and his sister Elizabeth. I hadn't eaten a thing for days and I couldn't make the pain go away. I glanced over to see my ex-wife, Joyce, and I couldn't help but feel her pain. Joyce was a good mother to my sons; she was in shock and couldn't stop crying.

My gaze was fixed on Deborah walking towards me with her usual determined gait. "Will (that is what she called me), would you want to be a pallbearer for Billy?" I was not quick to answer because I was not certain I was emotionally capable of this task. But I was touched that she thought enough of me to include me in this decision. This was a side of Deborah I had never seen, and I agreed.

Deborah came over and asked the pallbearers to wear Billy's uniform. Light-blue button-down shirts and khaki pants. A pallbearer for my own son! I had the most horrible feeling in the pit of my stomach while helping to carry him to his grave. Billy was always afraid of the dark, and now darkness would be his.

Losing a child is the most painful experience a parent can have. From the time the first car left the funeral home and arrived at St. John of God Church, the mile-long procession of cars were still leaving the funeral home. Mr. Musmanno said in 40 years in business, this was the biggest funeral he ever had. I made my way to the pew and had my eyes fixed on the casket. Father Regis Ryan conducted the service. Billy's cousin, Dean Panizzi, gave the eulogy. Dean and Billy were one month apart and grew up together. Nearly two months earlier, my son Gary's son died at 27. Before that, I had lost my youngest brother Ted, from a stroke at sixty-nine years old. Three people I loved died in one year. The words from the service flitted in and out of my head.

Father Ryan said, "The Power of God is more powerful than Oxi-Clean. It always has been; it always will be." When asked by reporters, Father Ryan said Billy believed in putting his talent to work, and he was not afraid to show the person he was. He went on to say, "We've been given talents too. We're called upon to use those talents even half as much as Billy did."

Now came the moment I dreaded. I helped carry my son Billy to his last resting place. As I walked alongside the casket, I knew this was the end. Outside, amidst the news reporters and TV cameras, we watched as Billy was placed in what was to be his last ride. It was raining by this time and we made our way to the Mt. Calvary Cemetery – a mile up the hill. As we walked to the tent set up for Billy, the sun shone through as we put the casket under the tent. Flowers were placed all around the casket. A gentle speaking man was there with doves. He gave each parent a feather from the dove. Very soothing music played as we gathered in a circle and then twenty doves were released. It brought peace while it lasted. We all needed that release and I appreciated the gesture.

After that, we gathered at Rockerfeller's in Kennedy Township to have a post-funeral gathering. This was the same place Little Billy's graduation party had been held. Deborah and her family were conspicuously absent, as they had left for the airport after the funeral service. I went through the motions of thanking people for coming, and what I really wanted was to go back to the cemetery and be near Billy privately. Instead, I focused my attention on my grandson (Billy Mays III). His girlfriend, Whitney, went back to Tampa and I wanted to spend some time with "Little Will." My son was proud of little Billy. He graduated from Full Sail University with a degree in music; little Billy is very talented in the music field. He made his own CD - where he sings, plays drums, and plays the guitar. I know little Billy will be someone famous someday. He already is well known, having been on the Discovery Channel with his dad. My dad played the violin so I think we passed the music gene along to him. Who knows? Maybe someday my grandson will have his own son and hopefully he will be a Billy Mays IV.

Billy's pallbearers: Me, Little Billy, Anthony Sullivan, Uncle
(maternal) Bobby, Dean, Ronnie, Kevin Farley

Celebrating Little Billy's graduation from Full Sail

NEW!

HI, I'M BILLY MAYS

IF YOU OWN A TELEVISION, YOU'VE ALREADY MET AMERICA'S GREATEST PITCHMAN

...get a package in ...ents—a gadget, a ...y did I buy this? ...only $19.95. It's ...'s's secret.
...D," Mays says. He ...'s the magic num- ...nknown item that ...e, that can be seen ...and that appeals ...o-it-yourselfers. ...from sheer quan-

...uger.com
...41-5744

Now recommend... OXICLEAN

...ays, here for OxiClean!" or ...hty Putty, Hercules Hook, ...er, Zorbeez, whatever. Mays ...gadgets that stick harder ...dig up weeds, hold up a 50- ...med mirror (assuming you ...nd gilt-framed mirror)—so ...s you never thought you ...even thought existed until ...to his pitch. A 30-second ...nore than two minutes—a ...aming at you, "Watch this! ...! I gotta tell you something! ...w!" So you call the toll-free ...a strange voice your credit-

IT'S NOT AS IF BILLY MAYS CAN SELL ANYTHING—JUST ALM GLO RICH, AND NOW, THANKS TO BILLY, OXICLEAN IS ON G SUCCESSFUL, IT POPS UP CHEAPER ON THE WEB AND BIL

tity. "I want to sell billions of things," he says. And he has, which has made him rich (three Bentleys, million-dollar homes) and famous. There are websites devoted to either loving or hating Billy Mays. He shrugs again and says, "There's a fine line between love and hate." One website is dedicated to fans who want to have his baby, though most of those fans are

gay call ket His of On he' sel ow of

to

s p a

P n d g

Chapter 5

Little Black Suitcase

As the week passed and this nightmare continued to unfold, I would see Billy's picture in the paper. Headlines about his death and even the details of funeral arrangements couldn't be kept private – it was all over the news. I was heartbroken and I tried to find solace in the mundane, everyday routine of things – walking my dog, pulling weeds in the vegetable garden, and harvesting and chopping the vegetables for some unknown recipe – cooking food that I couldn't bring myself to eat. And yet I continued to do something that I have always done ever since Billy became a public figure.

I was in the habit of cutting out articles and pictures of Billy from newspapers and magazines and keeping them together in a little collection so I could look at them whenever I wanted. My son traveled so much and was kept so busy that this was my way of keeping him close.

Whenever Billy sent me a card or a great photograph, I added it. My collection got too large for a scrapbook and it outgrew its cardboard box so I began using an old black suitcase on wheels that Billy had given me once when I was going home to Pittsburgh from visiting him. I could tuck it in the closet and pull it out whenever I had something else to add. Day after day, even though grief consumed me, I was diligent – neatly cutting out the pictures and text. I couldn't bear to read the words yet, but somehow this ritual of mine consoled me. As time passed, the sadness would come and go like waves on the ocean. Attempting to get lost in my work, the sheer routine of it helped slightly, but every morning when I pulled a fresh shirt out of the closet there was my black suitcase and all I had left of Billy.

My day started with a drive past the cemetery no matter what direction I was headed, and I usually stopped for a brief visit at Billy's grave. When the funeral arrangements were made, I was adamant about buying the plot next to him so that we could be buried together. Some mornings I would find flowers and even tubs of Oxi Clean, but I was always there with the same questions: Why did my charismatic son with the gift of gab have to die? Why did he have to leave me? Billy's death left such a void in my life – how would I ever fill it?

Because there is such a strong resemblance between myself and my son, people would walk up to me at the grocery store, at the gas station, and even on jobs to ask if I was Billy's dad and to express their condolences. Sometimes the cemetery was the only place I could find peace. I made his grave a garden and tended it religiously. Methodically, I scraped away the leaves, then loosened the soil and planted some plant or flower I picked up in my travels. This brought back memories of the boys bringing me tools as we worked in our family garden. I found comfort in my memories, and here I could talk to Billy and feel close to him. Shortly after Billy's death, I went to see my doctor because I couldn't shut off my mind, and despair overtook me. Even the antidepressants I was prescribed didn't help me as much as the freedom I felt to express myself there by Billy.

Death wasn't something new to me; it was part of me. A few months before Billy's death, my brother Teddy died at 69-years-old. Next, my 27-year-old grandson died suddenly. Then two weeks after Billy, my beloved companion of 18 years, Sammy, my beautiful black Pekingese left me. All this sadness within eight months. Sammy's death was the coup de gras. I cried like a child looking back at the departures of those so dear to me. My memories were my comfort. I needed to have a quiet time alone, just me and my little black suitcase. I carefully went through all the newspaper articles on Billy and the various magazines he was in. Playboy did an entire article on him along with so many other magazines. I also added all the photographs of Billy from childhood to his adult life. Lastly I added pictures of my buddy Sammy, pictures of those gone forever, and those precious memories that meant so very, very much to me. I had a dreadful dream one night that there had been a fire in my house and my little black suitcase was on fire and I was able to save it even though I had burns on my hands and face. That would have been a nightmare had it really happened! I pride myself in being a mature man of years of wisdom and common sense, but here I was, a 75 year-old man coveting a little black suitcase that meant the world to me in the dark days of my life.

Mays pitches reality show for Discovery

4-10-09

BY DAN NEIL
LOS ANGELES TIMES

Billy Mays sounds tired, which is a huge relief to me. I had braced myself for the onslaught of moon-barking enthusiasm the bearded pitchman brings to his direct-response TV ads for "OxiClean," "Kaboom," "Mighty Putty," the "Awesome Auger," the "Samurai Shark" sharpener.

The Mays in those ads seems to have the same problem as the de-hibernated Austin Powers, who can't control the volume of his voice.

The 50-year-old McKees Rock native has been on the road for three weeks promoting his new reality show, "Pitchmen," debuting Wednesday on the Discovery Channel.

After shilling dozens of products on zillions of two-minute commercials, Mays — the most successful direct-response salesman in TV history — is ready to breach into the pop-culture imperium.

And, so I ask the question that is top-of-mind whenever one first endures a Mays come-on: "Why so loud?"

"Over the years, we've tried it the other way, tried backing off," Mays says. "People will say, 'What's wrong with Billy?' We do the most in-your-face approach out there, because it works. You just have to look at the num...

'Pitchmen'

Premieres: 10 p.m. Wednesday on Discovery Channel

"We do the most in-your-face approach out there, because it works. You just have to look at the numbers."

BILLY MAYS
TV PITCHMAN AND HOST
OF DISCOVERY'S "PITCHMEN"

insinuation into every facet of their consciousness. Perhaps, consumers want to reward Mays for his refreshing lack of guile. An honest pitch deserves an honest sale, doesn't it?

Or, it could be Americans simply like to buy a lot of useful junk. A $19.95 chamois and "PedEggs" might be the recession-era methadone for cash-strapped shopaholics.

"Pitchmen," featuring Mays and fellow TV yell-and-seller Anthony Sullivan (of "Swivel Sweeper" fame), will follow the pair as they evaluate new products and make short-form infomercials f...

million– dollar bill

INFOMERCIAL GURU EXTRAORDINAIRE AND PITCHMAN STAR **BILLY MAYS** HAS MADE A FORTUNE HAWKING HOUSEHOLD CLEANERS AND COOKING SUPPLIES. WHAT'S NEXT FOR THIS ONE-MAN BRAND?

By Joseph Guinto | Illustration by QuickHoney

JUNE 15 2005 AMERICAN WAY 41

Billy's upbeat attitude and enthusiasm while pushing products made him an infomercial king

BILLY MAYS' speedy spiel and contagious enthusiasm made him an infomercial icon whose voice, face and bushy black beard were instantly recognized by millions of Americans.

Famed for pushing products like OxiClean stain remover, Orange Glo cleaner and Mighty Putty, beefy Mays was born in McKees Rocks, Pa., and played semi-pro football after graduating high school.

He was 24 when he stumbled upon the career that would make him rich, famous and a household name.

Watching a salesman hawk Ginsu knives on the boardwalk in Atlantic City, N.J., Mays was inspired to become a pitchman.

He honed his skills by studying other veterans of the pitchman's craft hustle their wares before small crowds.

Over the years, he and his co-star Anthony Sullivan racked up $1 billion in sales of products like cleaners, cookers and household aids.

But the super salesman insisted the key to success was not his machine-gun delivery, booming voice and trademark blue shirt – but the right products.

"You don't stay in this business as long as I have unless the products work," he said. "When I say, 'Billy Mays here for Mighty Putty,' all I have is my name and the trust of the audience.

"I would never let the consumer down."

Tragically, Mays was only 50 when his wife found him dead in his bed at their Tampa, Fla., home on June 28.

An autopsy found the father of a son and toddler daughter had an enlarged heart and was killed by a pulmonary embolism.

The infomercial king's career was still rocketing at the time of his passing. He'd expanded his product line to include insurance, was closing a deal with fast-food giant Taco Bell and was appearing on the reality show Pitchmen on the Discovery Channel.

Shortly before his death, he noted,

Billy Mays was perfect pitchman

Pallbearers wear Billy Mays' trademark blue shirt while carrying his

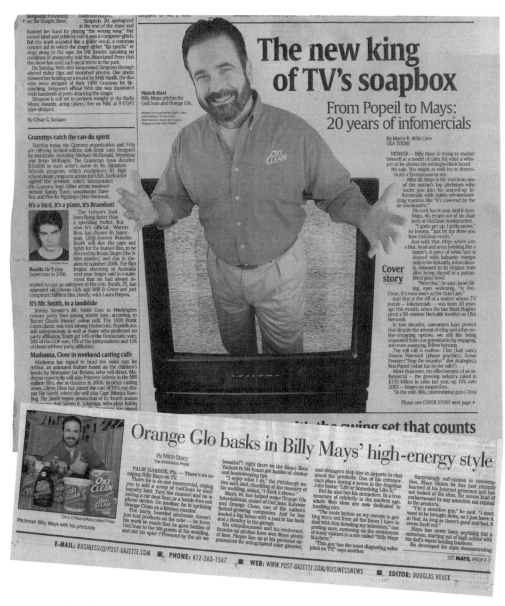

My Pekingese,
Sammy

From left: my grandson, Kyle, Billy with my grandaughter Elizabeth, and my grandson Gary with my great-grandson Juliano

Far left:
Gary and Juliano

Left:
Big brother, Juliano, with sister Lucy

Above: Billy with cousins Michael and Bobby. *Left:* Billy and Gary
Bottom Right: Billy

Chapter 6
My Son Billy

I found some childhood pictures of the boys in an old photo album and thought it would be a good idea to add them to my collection in the black suitcase. These are precious mementos, and they belong together. This picture was one of the first we had taken at a professional studio and they wore their Sunday best – little red suits and bowties. Every Sunday, the boys wore these suits to attend service at the Forest Grove Presbyterian Church. After church, we went home for Sunday dinner. When the boys changed, they would go out and play with their cousins, who would come to visit every Sunday. My sisters, their husbands, my brother Teddy, and his kids would all come over for dinner and spend the day. Billy, Gary, and Randy would play basketball, baseball, tag, and just run in the woods. They weren't entertained by video games – they used their imaginations. As they got older, I bought a horse and a pony. They also begged me for mini bikes and I ended up getting them the first ones with motors.

As they grew, so did their adventures. One summer in their early teens we had an opportunity to go the Canada with Ralph Bogatay, a friend of my father's from the police force. We drove to Toronto, got on a train with all of our gear, and went a thousand miles north to Georgian Bay, where we arrived at the outfitter's. We boarded 2 seaplanes that were provided by the outfitter and they took us to a 25,000 acre secluded lake with a log cabin with no electricity. The forest floor was like walking on a mattress because of the accumulation of pine needles. To keep our supplies cool, there was a deep hole for natural refrigeration. We were left there for a week with a radio in case of emergency. It was rugged, rustic, and fun. In the evenings, we would build a big fire and fry our catch of the day in an enormous iron skillet. You could see the northern lights from our fishing boats. Billy was in awe of the whole experience. Years later, the boys still talked about this vacation and Billy said he wanted to take his own children to see the northern lights.

The boys had such a great experience swimming and playing around in the lake that when we got back home, with the help of my brother Teddy, I built an in-ground pool that was 20 feet wide and 40 feet long. My sons were thrilled – it was the only pool like this in the whole area. Every chance they got, they would bring their friends and it was the neighborhood gathering spot. I loved to barbeque and watch them have fun – it kept them busy and I knew they were safe and off the streets. At the time, they were living with their mother in Ohio View Acres projects in McKees Rocks. We would go to the farm in Titusville, PA to hunt in the fall, and in the winter we had 2 snowmobiles we rode for miles and miles over the trails.

As the boys matured, they lost interest in going to the farm, and they wanted to spend more time with their friends. They also got interested in sports, thanks to their Uncle Cy, their mother's brother. I taught them to enjoy the outdoors and Cy taught them about team sports. Billy was addicted to working out – his dream was to become a football player. He lifted weights at the Boys and Girls Club of McKees Rocks. Billy's best childhood friend, Kevin Farley, said Billy was determined to become a football player and needed to add more weight, so he asked everyone in the cafeteria at school for their leftovers. He ended up becoming strong enough and eventually became Sto Rox MVP as a linebacker. To this day, some of the records that he held still haven't been broken. When the boys were in high school, I promised each of them a car upon graduation. Not only were we generations apart, but the way I raised my boys was totally different from the way I was raised.

I grew up in Robinson Township, Pennsylvania on seven acres of land that my father William B. Mays bought from his brother Alex. My dad bought the land in 1932 after my brother Luama was born. My brother Lu was born at my grandmother's house that was referred to as the "Crows Nest" because it was so remote and situated deep in the thick woods. The rest of us were all born at home on Phillips Lane, in our house that was built by my dad with the help of his father-in-law. I was born March 3, 1936 and a baby came along every year after that. My sister, Faye, was born next in 1937, followed by Bob in '38, then Ruth in '39 and baby Teddy in '40.

Our house had a basement kitchen, where my mother would cook on a woodstove. I can still smell the aroma of the huge cherry-filled cookies she would bake with cherries from the tree in the backyard. A living room was off to the left of the kitchen and it would always be warm and cozy with the heat of the woodstove. My mother was especially creative in keeping us all fed and clothed. Growing up during the depression was quite an experience, compared to what kids have today. It was an education in itself. As you went up the stairs, shoes would be lined up on each step. My mother would say, "Pick up your shoes and take them upstairs." We valued our shoes because we only had one pair. My mother would carefully clean and polish our shoes each night. Upstairs, we had two bedrooms, one for my parents and one for us kids. The children's room had three beds – one for the two girls and two beds for the four boys. On a hot summer night we would sneak outside and sleep on the slanted roof of the root cellar. That roof gave us relief from the stifling heat and a view of the stars.

We had no indoor plumbing in those days. It is hard to imagine going outside to an outhouse for a bathroom, but that's just what we did! There was also a springhouse on the property that was a storehouse built over a spring and that kept the food cold. We all carried water from the springhouse in galvanized buckets for cooking, cleaning, and the weekly bath in a washtub. My mother made fresh butter from our own cow's milk in the shelter of the cool springhouse. We must have been very poor since this was the time of the Great

Depression, but I never felt that way. My parents worked the land and raised chickens, cows, and pigs for food and income.

Summers were spent hoeing corn and tomatoes, feeding pigs, cows, and chickens and cleaning pens. We would butcher pigs and chickens, make sausage, harvest eggs and produce, which my father would sell door to door in an area where, coincidentally, I currently reside. Then there was the planting of four to five thousand tomato plants by hand. Our big Belgian gelding, Charlie, would pull a plow to make a row and we would follow behind him putting a handful of horse manure and a tomato plant every foot or so along the row. How I loved that horse! My father bought him from a farm in Bellevue, PA and our neighbor rode him home because we didn't have access to a horse trailer. Our neighbor Chuck was quite the horseman because it was about a twelve-mile ride and he had to coax the huge horse over the mile-long McKees Rocks Bridge over the Ohio River. Horses can spook easily and that bridge is quite high. Charlie was a huge workhorse, sorrel in color with a flaxen mane, tail, and fetlocks. I have fond memories of straddling across his wide back while my dad led him through the fields.

On a hot summer afternoon, we would all beg our parents to let up from the chores so we could go swimming in Montour Creek. We would dive off an old concrete wall left over from the railroad. We never had any swimming lessons; we taught each other how to swim. When the tomatoes had ripened, they'd be harvested and sold, and my mother would also can them with the help of her mother-in-law, Anna. She canned over 100 quarts of tomatoes that would feed all of us for the winter. Life was hardest in the winter. I had to get up early to milk a cow for our milk before I went to school every day. After school, it was more milking, cleaning stalls, feeding animals, and gathering eggs. We were self-sufficient on the farm. All we had to purchase was sugar, flour, and lard from the Economy Market in McKees Rocks.

My father would work odd jobs to provide for us when necessary. Back in the early 40s with six kids to feed, he had his work cut out for him. He was willing to do anything, whatever it took to survive. I remember him driving a bus for the Montour School District in Robinson, where my siblings and I attended school. My dad also worked for the South Penn Oil Company, where his hand was severely cut open and was stitched back together. After that, he couldn't open his hand all the way. My earliest recollection of his hand is that it was like a claw, and it was his right hand as well. He wasn't handicapped though – he dealt with it. He could no longer work at the oil company so he worked part-time in a little coal mine he started on his mother's property. The coal he mined he sold to folks to heat their homes. Later in life, my father eventually became a Robinson Township police officer. I often thought that he was thinking ahead so that he could provide some sort of retirement for my mother and our family. A policeman's pension and health insurance gave her the security that a farmer's life could not.

As for me, my childhood was spent happily outdoors exploring the woods after I was finished with my chores. I feel sorry for today's youth because they lack the freedom we had as kids. I had a trap line set with traps to catch mink or muskrats along what is now the Montour Trail in Robinson Township. I would get up extra early and run down into the hollow along the creek to see if I had caught anything. Once I trapped an animal, I would skin it, rub salt on the skin, and wait for it to dry. I learned this technique from my father, who also trapped as a boy. Once the skin had completely dried, I would wrap it in brown paper and send it to the Wilson Fur Company. Usually I would get about one dollar and fifty cents to three dollars for a pelt. One time I was lucky enough to trap a mink and I received thirty dollars for it! That was a fortune to me back then. When I handed the money to my father as my contribution to the family, he put his hands on my shoulders and he said, "Good job, son! I'm proud of you."

The first time I was ever away from home was my first day of school. Naturally, I was very scared when my dad dropped me off, and it was also the time I got an inkling that some people lived differently than we did. When we left for school in the morning, our mother had lunches all wrapped in the *Sunday Sun Telegraph* newspaper and tied up with string. In the little bundle would be sandwiches on homemade bread filled with baked beans, or fresh pork if we were lucky. Every time I taste a Concord grape, it takes me back to lunchtime at school because my mother always put grapes from the grape arbor or a seckel pear from the tree in our lunch. I couldn't help but notice that some kids and our teacher (we all ate together in those days) had store bought sliced bread for their sandwiches. I often coveted that because I didn't have it. One day, my teacher asked me to trade lunches with her. I thought she was being kind to me, but she said she hadn't had homemade bread in so long – she really missed the taste and texture of it. Baked bean sandwiches reminded her of home and her mother. I was happy to trade but soon realized I wasn't missing anything, and I gained an appreciation for all that my mother did for us.

My mother was a sensitive, loving woman, and when she looked into your eyes you understood that she knew a lot about life. I can still remember her telling the story about her brother, Victor, running to the pond and pulling out his dead child. The whole family was down at the pond rinsing off vegetables they had just picked to get them ready for market. Victor and his wife turned their backs for a minute – just enough time for the two-year-old Louise to slip into the water and drown. Victor was wailing as he held the lifeless two-year-old to his chest. Closer, closer he held her and he wouldn't let her go. "Gone!" Mom said, "and that was the death of Victor too, because he was never the same after that. Everyone who knew him said he was a walking dead man." You would think that was enough tragedy for one family, but unfortunately, it didn't stop there. My mother's sister, Bertha, also lost her daughter, Valera, at eighteen months of age after she tripped and fell head first into a tub of water. While playing baseball, an errant bat killed my dad's brother Philander, at 7 years old. While the family was gathered for a summer outing at the farm, the young boys were playing baseball out in a field. The lad smacked the ball and the bat swung back and smashed Philander, who was catching, in the head. Blood splattered everywhere and the boys were screaming for their parents. By the time they could get medical attention, Philander was dead. Gone! Another member of the Mays family beset by tragedy; Dad said after that no one could enjoy outings at the farm. The echoes of the heart wrenching screams could be heard for years to come. The farm was sold because of this, and Dad hung his head in disbelief that such a tragedy had struck our family once again.

I wish I could say that death ended here, but of course, it did not. Philander Mays Sr., my grandfather, came down with TB and after a valiant fight, succumbed to it. Left alone, my grandmother, Anna, had to figure out a way to raise my father, William, and his brother, Alex. It wasn't easy in those days, a woman alone, but Anna did the best she could, picking up odd jobs washing and ironing. There were no hospitals for childbirth; most babies were born at home with assistance from family members. Word spread that there was a doctor, Dr. Burkett, who became well known in the area for his skill with obstetrics. He was kept quite busy and eventually needed someone to assist as a midwife for women whose labor was progressing. My Grandma Anna met Dr. Burkett while helping with the delivery of a neighbor. Anna was so calm and attentive to her friend that the doctor offered her a job as his assistant. This was a godsend for my grandmother, who had two sons to feed. The two traveled by horse and buggy in those days, doing their best to make haste to house calls. I recall a family story about Anna leaving the doctor at one home while she traveled to another farm with a mother –to-be in distress. The horse had other ideas and took Anna for a wild ride through the countryside until she could dislodge the horse's bit, which it held between its teeth.

When a horse clenches the bit in its teeth, it is like driving a car without brakes; you can't stop it! Anna was terrified with the runaway horse and buggy, but adrenaline must have kicked in and given her the strength to gain control. She arrived at her destination safe but disheveled, with her long, gray hair hanging to her shoulders on one side as it fell out of her usually meticulously groomed, tight bun. You never saw my grandmother Anna's hair down, except at bedtime.

As Anna burst into the house, the birth mother cried out, "Thank God you are here!" It was as though the baby waited for her arrival, because she then delivered a healthy baby boy. Those that didn't have money to pay Anna for her services often gave her what they could. She would bring home chickens, eggs, homemade preserves, baked goods, and homemade quilts – any item that might help her family. Our family survived these losses through perseverance and faith. I never related to these stories until I had my own cross to bear.

My older brother, Lu, was drafted into the army after high school. I wanted to quit school in 10th grade, but my father wouldn't let me. He convinced me to go to a trade school. I decided I wanted to become a bricklayer, so I went to Connelly Trade School for 2 years. Today, I am glad I took his advice. Of my younger two brothers Bob and Ted, my parents struggled to put Bob through college, while Ted would go on to become a helicopter mechanic.

I didn't use my trade, however, until some years later. I was more interested in trucks, which led me in a different direction. After trade school at

17, I started operating an old 1946 International dump truck and a Case farm tractor with a front loader. I would haul fill and topsoil for new homes that were being built. Back then I would get $3.00 a load for fill and $10 a load for topsoil. I loved what I was doing and spent seven days a week doing it. Eventually, Lu went into the army and left the truck behind for me to use.

I was driving truck one summer for my cousin at Phillips Contracting, hauling a coal by-product in a big tractor-trailer. It was hot, I had the window down, and I was enjoying the warm breeze from a summer afternoon. Even over the groans of the truck's engine, I could hear the chirping of the birds. I'll never forget the first time I saw her standing on the street corner. The sight of this pretty, young gal standing there in shorts and a top, showing off her fleshy curves made me want to pull over right then and there. I wanted to meet that gal with the long black hair, but I wondered how I'd ever be able to overcome my painful shyness to say hello. Back at home, I was telling my younger sister about my plight. As fate would have it, she knew the girl. "Joyce works with me at the Vaseline plant," Faye said. "I'll introduce you properly when you pick me up at work tomorrow." Faye was as good as her word, and eventually we had that first date that led to several dates.

Our nights were often spent with my sister Faye, and her husband, Bud. At that time, I owned a jet-black Chevy convertible with red leather seats. Damn, I was hot back then! We made some lasting memories in my Chevy. It was not long after that that Joyce told me she was pregnant. I know Billy was conceived right there in the front seat of that car. In fact, I remember the exact night. We were barely out of our teens and about to become parents. I did what you did in those days – marry the girl and take responsibility. We were married at the Union Presbyterian Church in Robinson Township, where I attended church and Sunday school as a child. A small reception followed at my parent's house. There was no honeymoon; we just started our lives together.

My Mother's Family.
Top: Bob, Mike, Vic
Middle: Bertha, Katherine, Elizabeth, Tillie, Lena *Bottom:* Gretchen and Peter

My grandparents, Peter and Gretchen

My brothers and I with our sister and a neighbor girl
From left: Lu, Lucy (neighbor), me, Faye, and Bob

Striking a pose with
my 1956 Ford Pickup

My 1957 Chevy
Convertible. This is where
Billy was concieved.

My son, Billy

Gary, Randy, and Billy

Billy

Billy and Gary

From right: Gary, Randy, Billy, Janie, Michael, Bobby, and a neighbor at my mother's house

Fishing at the farm in Titusville

Randy   Gary

Billy with my sister, his Aunt Ruth

Billy and Uncle Cy

My family. *From left:* Me, William Benton (Dad), Ted, Lena (Mom), Ruth, Lu, Faye and Bob

With my grandsons, Zack and Billy III

Billy, Dee Dee, and little Billy with Joyce's side of the family

Joyce

Joyce with Uncle Rich Panizzi

Chapter 7
Early Years

I was thinking of all the things that Billy had accomplished and how far he had come and I pulled out the picture of our first apartment. Everything that was important to me I've lost. Billy was born when I was twenty-two years old and my wife Joyce just nineteen. We lived in a modest apartment in Piddock, Pennsylvania, a tiny town with just a grocery store and a post office in lower McKees Rocks. The town of McKees Rocks is located on the Ohio River, three miles west of the point at Pittsburgh, PA, where the Allegheny and Monongahela Rivers meet to form the mighty Ohio.

The town has a colorful history and there are several theories as to how it got its name. Indians built a burial mound on top of a rocky bluff that settlers used as a point of reference. It became known as McKees Rocks Mound, so some think the name was derived from the burial ground. Alexander McKee owned most of the land in the area by the time he hosted George Washington in his eight-room log home in 1770, so some feel this is how the town got its name. No one disputes the fact that it was built by the hard work and sweat of German, Italian, Russian, and other immigrants.

The Pennsylvania and Lake Erie Railroad made McKees Rocks its hub and had a repair and maintenance facility there. Many factories found the location desirable as well, due to the availability of the railroad and the river. This is also where the Jenny Lee and Mancini bakeries were founded, along with Trap's Bar (whose owner had a pet monkey that sat on his shoulder in the bar) and Mann's hotel.

The latter, Mann's hotel, had the distinction of being named a historical landmark because it was a noted stagecoach stop, a jail, and, during the Civil War, an official post office stop for the Pony Express. Most people remember it for its famous turtle soup! The Mann's hotel was the longest continually operated business in McKees Rocks, having been opened from 1803 until 1991. People had been trying to save it and keep it from being demolished, but the town unexpectedly demolished Mann's hotel in the early morning hours in 2009 without any warning. Still, if you ask most people in McKees Rocks, they have a story about the place.

Our apartment was on the second floor, in a building located near Joyce's mother's house, and rent was a whopping twenty-eight dollars a month. Our home had a small eat-in kitchen, a tiny bedroom in an alcove with a crib, and a living room where Joyce and I slept on a sofa bed. Obviously, times were tough back then. There were no Bentleys in the garage – just an old dump truck I used for landscaping. One year to the day after Billy's birth, son number two, Gary, was born. I was determined to make a better life for my young family and I always dreamt of starting my own business and working for myself. I hauled topsoil, but it was especially hard in the winter when the ground was frozen. I tried stripping coal for a couple of years, but that didn't work out very well. Son number three, Randy, was born on Dec. 8, 1960.

I had a dream of us all working together someday. All of the hard work paid off financially, but on the home front my wife felt neglected and the responsibility of three small boys took its toll. Joyce said I was never home, but I showed my love by working and providing the best life I could. Many nights I would drag home, just wanting a hot shower and to fall into bed, but instead I was met with a barrage of accusations from Joyce's frustrations of being both a mother and father to the boys.

Eventually, this led to the breakup of a very short marriage. As I approached the judge, she asked Joyce why she wanted a divorce. "He works too much and he's *never* home," she replied. The judge seemed compassionate and tried to explain to my wife that there could be worse things than a hard working man, but Joyce glared at me and said, "You're nothing but a dumb farmer – you'll never amount to anything." Those words will stay with me forever, and she actually did me a favor. That always spurred me on to work harder to prove her wrong. Even though I added three more trucks and a bulldozer, winters came and I couldn't make a living. I went back to hauling dirt in the day and driving a truck in the city at night.

I loved working outdoors – it was hard work but very rewarding and I enjoyed seeing a job take shape, but with a young family to provide for, I was forced to find work that wasn't seasonal. An offer came from Refuse Systems to haul refuse at night. The job wasn't conducive to family life, but it did provide. For three years, I discovered a different side of Pittsburgh at night. One hot summer evening I remember approaching a dumpster to empty it, and suddenly up popped the head of a man. He shook his fist and shouted obscenities at me as he jumped out of the dumpster. He was a mill worker who thought he'd catch a quick nap and hide away from the boss by sleeping in there. It scared me to think I might've crushed him to death in the back of my truck!

In those days, Pittsburgh was a booming steel city. Blast furnaces belching and the stench of sulfur filling the air. To this day, hard-boiled eggs remind me of that odor. The South Side was home to J & L Steel and was only busy between shifts of lunch-pail carrying, blue-collar workers. It didn't have any upscale bars and restaurants and pricey real estate. My job was to pick up industrial refuse all over the city. Banding shops had large containers filled with scrap material they discarded after making rolls of steel used to manufacture appliances and automobiles.

One rainy night, I was headed up Green Tree Hill carrying a full load of refuse for the landfill in Imperial, PA. I saw lights in my mirror and then they disappeared and I felt a thump. A VW bug had run into the back of the garbage truck and went underneath it! A young woman in a steward-ess uniform was inside crying hysterically. "Please. Move my car before the police come!" I could tell she was very inebriated and kept repeating over and over that she could lose her job if the police found her drunk. It was her boyfriend's new car and all she kept begging me to do was pick up her car with the arms of my garbage truck. She was so drunk she thought I was a tow-truck driver, and there was no reasoning with her. Luckily, I had my two-way radio and promptly called my dispatch and asked him to call the police. I then proceeded to set up flares and had her go to the side of the road with her car after myself and two other men pushed it over to the berm. I made sure she was safe and headed for the dump. Other than these few, strange incidents and the occasional rat crawling up out of the refuse, it was lonely and monotonous but it was a steady income.

Hard work finally paid off and I had the chance to do something on my own again. Allegheny Disposal, a refuse company, became available and I was able to buy it from Randy Honeywell. I could visualize our family business in my mind: W.D. Mays and Sons, Inc.

The boys were getting a little older and I made sure I made the most of my time with them. Weekends were special – my sons loved fishing. Billy, his brothers, and my nephew Mike loved to go on fishing trips to Canada and Cape May or go up to the farm. Since Joyce was staying home to raise the kids, I was the sole source of support for her and the boys, until they turned eighteen. Joyce didn't have a car, so I bought a nice convertible for her to drive. We tried to get along for the sake of the children, as most divorced parents do. As a young man, I felt I had to put my personal life on hold. Dates were for weekdays - weekends were for the boys.

The business began to take off, and Mays and Sons was now hauling refuse for many major industrial companies in the Pittsburgh area. The work was beginning to be too much for one man. In June of 1972 I got a wake-up call. I was so tired coming home after a long day that I didn't hear the train when I was crossing a railroad track. The train was moving backwards and just caught the back of the truck and turned it over. Feeling dizzy and feeling a warm trickle of blood run down my face I wondered, is this how all my hard work would end? Miraculously, a doctor witnessed the accident and attended to me. Eventually an ambulance arrived and took me to the hospital, and I was lucky only to have sustained a concussion and cuts to the face.

I knew I needed help, but whom could I trust to help me? My youngest brother, Ted, was a hard worker, and after the accident I asked him if he would be interested in working with me. He quit his job as an elevator mechanic for Westinghouse and started working at the business. Ted's wife Mary Jane eventually became the bookkeeper, and so it was a real family enterprise. Ted's friend, Tom Nolan, answered the phones and dispatched the drivers. We now had 5 or 6 drivers working and 8 trucks. This was a business built on sweat and sacrifice, but things were beginning to pay off in a big way.

The business was growing faster than I could keep up with it. I also faced the loss of my father at this time. My sons and I were enjoying the day at White Swan Park, a local amusement park. On the way home we passed an ambulance and emergency vehicles in front of the Brothers Grimm tavern. Little did I know, my father was answering a call about a disturbance on the premises when he suffered a massive heart attack and died on the scene. I didn't find out about this until I got home and my mother rushed outside to break the bad news. My mother was alone then and I so wanted to bring the family back together again. After my brother Bob graduated from the University of Pittsburgh, he was employed by Dupont in Baltimore, but eventually made his way to California. There he left engineering and began making money turning over houses in La Jolla, CA.

Bob came home for a visit and witnessed what was going on. Our business was thriving and I was able to afford improvements to the family home and the in-ground swimming pool for the boys and our family to enjoy. Thinking back on it now, I remember Bob had some kind of look in his eyes. Was it jealousy or envy? I think Bob decided right then and there to get in on it. Although Bob was successful in real estate, after the break-up of his marriage, he wanted to come home. Bob was different, worldly, but he wouldn't look you in the eye. He was a glutton as a child and always thought he should have more than the rest of us. He was sickly growing up, so my parents felt sorry for him and let him get away with it. Maybe this is why when I talked to Teddy about making Bob a partner, he wasn't too keen on the idea. I had my suspicions about why he wanted to move back home, but, after all, if you can't trust your brother, who can you trust?

And so it was, the end of W.D. Mays & Sons and the birth of Mays Corp. I divided my business up into 3 equal parts and I thought that was only fair since we were all family. This was to become Billy Mays first sales position – where he cut his teeth. Billy enrolled at West Virginia University with the hopes of eventually becoming a walk-on and possibly gaining a football scholarship but realized it wasn't what he wanted. Soon after that, he became even more discouraged with poor grades, and after an incident where he snuck a girl into his dorm room and got disciplined, he dropped out altogether. I became vice president of sales for Mays Corp. He came home and he and I became a father and son sales force, looking for new accounts and disposal sites. Teddy was in charge of the day-to-day operations, the trucks, the mechanics and the drivers. He was also in charge of the maintenance of the garage, which had expanded to a terminal in Imperial, PA.

Ted and I really didn't know what to do with Bob. He really didn't know anything about trucks or the trucking business, but he did have a college education. Bob wanted to be president of the company so he could stay in the office and take charge of running the operation on that end. Eventually he hired his friend Mike Stubna to be the company attorney. A red flag should have gone up when Bob pushed Mary Jane out and took care of the books himself. Tom Nolan was the next to go. Bob had total control! When we made him president, he actually believed in his mind that he owned the company. Over Bombay martinis at our favorite local bar and restaurant he was overheard by my old friends and business associates as saying, "I am going to own that company someday." But Ted and I dismissed their warnings. We just thought his arrogance was brought on by too much alcohol.

The business continued to grow and Bob wanted to diversify and invest in property. With his real estate background, we took his advice and purchased over one hundred acres of commercial property in the late 1970s and early 80s. The property was located in Imperial, PA near the interstate, Robinson Twp, Route 60 and Oakdale, PA. It's hard to believe that I was oblivious to what was going on around me, but I had complete trust in my brothers. Little did I know that in Bob's devious mind, he was buying the properties for himself.

Bob Mays and Mike Stubna formed a company called Mays Properties; it was a company built on greed and my own brother's insatiable appetite for more. Mays Properties had Bob Mays listed as the president, vice president, secretary, and treasurer and Mike as assistant secretary. Five days later, they transferred all of the properties owned by Mays Corp. over to Mays Properties for a couple thousand dollars, my brother's weekly salary. The notary responsible was none other than Mike's wife Christine. Then Bob intentionally and single-handedly bankrupted Mays Corp.

This wasn't the first time Bob was doing questionable things to undermine the company I had worked so hard to build up. To no knowledge of my own, he started dumping barrels at illegal dumpsites in the middle of the night. Eventually he was caught and when he was confronted by officials demanding he remove the barrels and eventually appeared in court, he would prepare by dressing up like a farmer, not bathe for several days, roll around in hay to make it look like he lived in a barn, and he even went so far as to take out his front partial. In front of the judge, Bob acted like a simple farmer, cried and quoted Bible verses! His lack of compliance forced the Dept. of Environmental Resources to deny our application for a license to haul. As a result, we couldn't haul any more industrial refuse and lost most of our major accounts. This forced the bankruptcy of Mays Corp. and got it out of Bob's way, as he never wanted anything to do with trucks anyway. Bob had a habit to feed just like a drug addict. He still needed more.

Ted informed me he began selling equipment that was financed and reneging on bank loans. Bob thought his job was getting money from the banks and the banker's job was to get it back. When he refused to pay a loan and the banker challenged him he would say, "Don't take it personally – it's just business!" No contract could ever be as binding as my handshake. I was always on a first name basis with my banker and my credit was impeccable because I was adamant about paying back my loans. Bob had a much different business plan. His idea was to borrow as much money from the bank as he could with no intention of repaying it.

Bob actually changed the company's phone number when his ex wife would call for money he owed her. What little clients we had left couldn't find us either! Bob finally moved his office from the terminal to the Route 60 property. Ted and I just thought he was crazy but he wanted all of the privacy to do what he wanted, get total control of what was left.

Me at 17 with my first truck, a 1946 International Dumptruck

Fishing in Canada

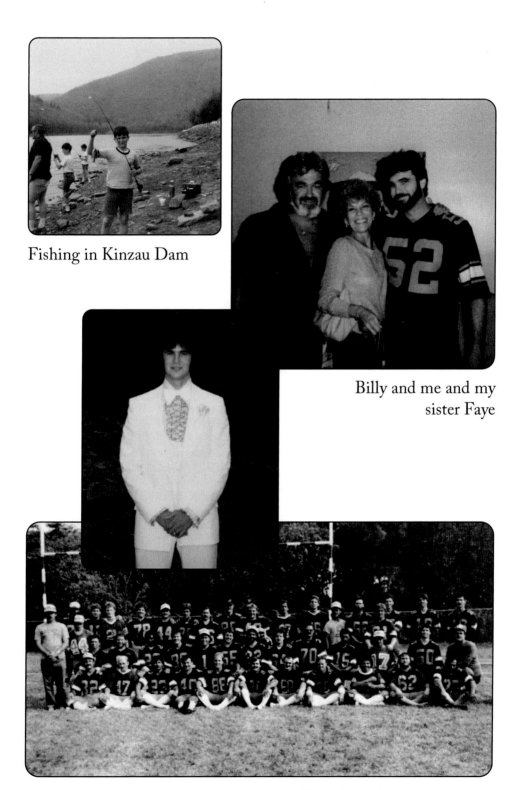

Fishing in Kinzau Dam

Billy and me and my
sister Faye

Billy and the Sto-Rox Rangers

Chapter 8

A Chance to Cash Out

I n the late 70s when Mays Corp was at its peak, Browning Ferris Industries (BFI), an international refuse company, offered the partners one million dollars for the company. In addition to the buyout, they wanted to hire all three partners with salaries and benefits to continue operations before BFI completely took it over.

We met at the former Johnny Lounders restaurant in Robinson Township, PA with the principles from BFI. I remember thinking, as I was driving over there, "I wonder what my next venture is going to be..." My intent was to go to the farm in Venango County near Titusville and start an organic farm. That was my weekend retreat and I wanted to make it my permanent home. It was tranquil there which I realized when I was out in the field mowing on my Farmall tractor, which was probably the reason my father bought it in the first place. The plan was in place; all I needed was the capital to get started.

When I arrived at the restaurant, my brothers and the BFI executives were already inside. I nodded to the bartender, Butch, to send over my usual drink and shook hands with the prospective buyers in hopes that this whole thing would be finished tonight and I could start the next chapter in my life. Bob had his arms folded in front of him, and I could tell by his body language that his mind was already made up.

Since I had given Ted his third of the company, I thought Teddy would go along with me, but Bob had already convinced him otherwise not to sell. The company was grossing about one million dollars then but Bob felt we would make far more money in the future with the property we owned.

I wanted to sell while we were on top and I was saddened that Teddy's loyalty was with Bob. Majority ruled and Bob turned BFI down. In hindsight, I now know why Bob didn't want to sell to BFI. He didn't want to share the profits he'd calculated he'd earn when he took over everything for himself.

I've got to say, I've never forgiven my brother for what he ultimately did to Teddy and me, and the way that he fractured our family—but one good thing did come from Bob – his son Peter. Peter is nothing like his dad, and at least we talk every now and then. Since Peter is a good man, I've taken a lesson from that whole experience: don't judge a son by the actions of the father.

If you're wondering why I didn't bring my brother to justice, I couldn't wrap myself around the thought he could betray me. In my heart, I just couldn't believe he was capable of destroying everything I had worked so hard to build from the ground up. It took me thirty years to build and build, and Bob a year and a half to destroy. When I think back, I wouldn't change a thing. In retrospect, I know everything happens for a reason. My business demise forced Billy to find a new path.

I really liked working with my family, and I believe in destiny. I knew how to work hard and make money but was overwhelmed with the demands of the busines. I should have hired someone to advise me. I should have insisted that two signatures be required on company checks as a precaution, but I didn't. What happened, I let happen. All along, I thought Bob would sell the properties eventually and share the profits with Ted and me. Only after the statute of limitations ran out and I was told from an independent attorney Ted and I hired, did I believe what Bob was capable of doing to me.

I read an article in an airplane magazine that talked about the demise of my company. Billy was interviewed and was quoted as saying, "the business fizzled." This is what happens when someone dies and leaves you – you can't set the record straight. I'm sure wherever Billy is, he knows this. My brother Bob wanted the business to fail so it would be out of the way. The property is what he wanted and he didn't care who or what he destroyed in the process.

The only thing I retained from that whole mess was the Venango farm property that was our family legacy. My father purchased 30 acres with the dream of retiring there. He never lived to see his dream fulfilled because in 1972 he died while on duty as a policeman, yet another untimely death in the Mays lineage.

I found myself wanting to be up at the farm more and more. The farm gave me the feeling of serenity, and I felt safe there. When the boys were growing up, I would pack them up and head North. This was our escape and we enjoyed the freedom it provided. Together we built a pond and it became our favorite fishing spot. In the fall, the farm became our hunting camp. Since I took such an interest in the place, my mother suggested that I purchase it from her so I could pass it down to the boys. I was able to do that and enjoy it for a time, but that would not last. One of my deepest regrets in life is that I had to eventually sell my beloved farm. After I lost everything, I had no choice but to liquidate the farm for cash since I was flat broke. The only consolation was that I sold the property for thirty thousand dollars and I was able to live off of that for a few years.

Little did I know at that time that our ancestors lived in the surrounding area. Maybe that is why my father was drawn to the property in the first place. My older brother, Lu, uncovered this connection while researching our ancestry. My father, William Benton Mays, was named after Major William Benton Mays, who served and ultimately died during the Civil War.

Col. W. B. Mays

Left: Gravestones in Oil City for Loammi, Alpheus, and W.B. Mays

Chapter 9
Mays Men in the Service

I found a large manila envelope at the bottom of my suitcase. I didn't remember what was in it and as I opened it, I saw a really old picture of William Benton Mays in uniform. One impressive fact about my line of the Mays name is that the Mays men and their families have been a part of the American dream since before the Revolutionary War and have served the nation in every war since.

Johan (or John?) Mays was a flatboat river captain who transported people and supplies. It is funny to think he most likely passed through Pittsburgh and right by McKees Rocks on his way to seek his fame and fortune. He was killed in a battle with Indians when he was carrying new settlers to Limestone. He was so popular with village inhabitants and his courage in fighting off the Indians was appreciated so much, the townspeople renamed the village of Limestone "Maysville." The port of entry of Maysville, KY is one of the oldest landing places on the Ohio River. Maysville was and still is famous for its bituminous quarries. Some would say Maysville is also famous for its Daniel Boone Tavern and several of his family who are buried in the Maysville Cemetery.

The earliest Mays boy to serve his country was Thomas Mays, who served during the Revolutionary War as a private in John McClure's South Carolina Mounted Riflemen at the Battle of Hanging Rock and the Battle of Camden, S.C. His grandson, Thomas Washington Mays, served in the War of 1812 in the 132nd regiment.

During the American Civil War, many men of the Mays family served the Union. Notably, William Benton Mays of the Fourth Pennsylvania Cavalry, who was killed by a sniper on April 7th, 1863 at the age of 28, was awarded the rank of Colonel upon his death. His brother Loammi (age 24) was killed at Stony Creek, and their brother Corporal Alpheus served in the Civil War until his death in 1864 at the age of 21. Philander Alexander Mays (the third out of the four brothers to serve) would also see much action and was the only one to make it through the war and come home.

I can't help but think about those four Mays men that fought for their country. That three out of the four Mays boys would not survive and that for some reason God saw fit to let Philander go on to meet and marry Sara Jane Wilkins and live his life out is something I can't help but be thankful for. If he hadn't survived that bloody war, my line of the Mays family would never have existed!

After serving their country, the Mays men remained in service in their communities as: farmers, businessmen, and tradesmen. Some went into coal and oil. Others became lawyers and judges, such as Judge Karnes, descendent of Henry C. Mays 1812-1883.

The most recent Mays to have served his country is my brother Luama W. Mays. In 1956 the President by act of Congress presented Lu (warrant officer junior grade) the Distinguished Flying Cross for heroism in May 1955. While flying an army helicopter in Greenland on an assigned mission on May 11, Lu Mays and two other pilots were suddenly engulfed in a white out. A white out is a snow fog so dense the pilot cannot see the ground or the sky. Since the copter he was flying had inadequate instruments, he couldn't use them for orientation. It was his extensive flying experience that allowed him to land. Two other copters crashed, killing one pilot and injuring another man. Lu Mays managed to aid those personnel uninjured and deliver them to shelter and was able to report and direct the rescuers to the crash site.

My brother Lu now lives in Cincinnati. He earned a degree in education from the University of Omaha, then went on to the University of Cincinnati law school and became a lawyer. He received a Medal of Valor at the Soldiers and Sailors Hall in Pittsburgh in March 2011.

One of the most ironic connections we found out about all of these Mays men came generations later, when we found out well after the property was purchased and the house was built, that Billy's house in Greenville, SC was within close proximity of where William Benton Mays fought a battle during the Civil War!

A Civil War memorial in Franklin, PA

OUR MAYS ANCESTORY
Thomas Washington Mays Line

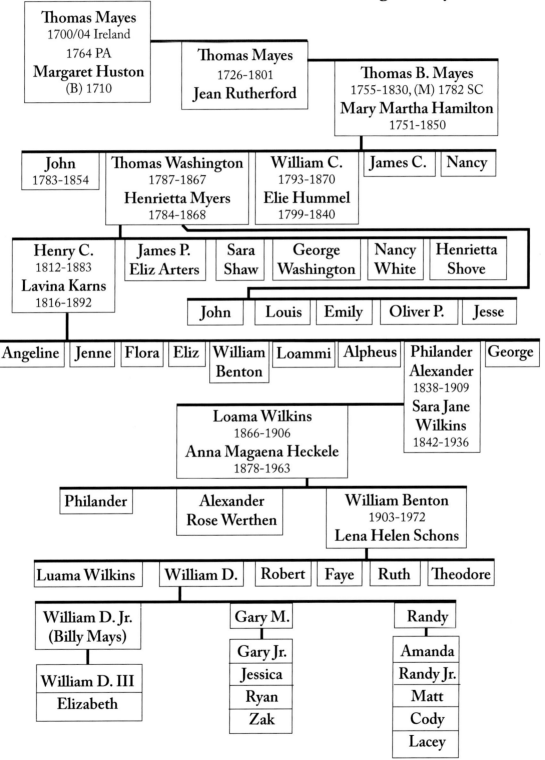

Chapter 10
Atlantic City, Cincinnati, & My Marriage to Kathy

Paper-clipped to the back of the envelope was a picture of my two brothers and Billy. After the decline of my business due to the deception of my greedy brother, Bob, Billy and I found ourselves in similar situations. We were both suddenly out of a job we'd grown to love, and by the hands of a Mays man no less. We had hit rock bottom and had to start over with nothing. I was reduced to moving to Cincinnati and working for my brother, Lu, and Billy found his way to Atlantic City, NJ.

It's funny how certain events that seem bad at the time can actually be the moments that change our lives for the better. Of course, we have no way of knowing this at the time, and I think there's a reason for it. We have to go through these times of trouble in order to push us in new directions, to help us learn the lessons we need to in this life to move us towards becoming better people. Both Billy and I were going in different directions because of need, and little did either one of us know where the heck we'd end up. Thinking back now and remembering that crazy story about how Billy ended up going to Atlantic

City, I have to laugh about it. Life is so full of surprises - I've learned you never look a gift horse in the mouth.

It was one of those nights when Dee Dee was working late hours at the shoe store that Billy decided to have a few guys over for beers. I often think Billy could have been a comedian because he liked nothing more than cracking up his friends with his one-liners! This particular evening, after several hours of drinking around the kitchen table, the party escalated. His hysterical buddies were falling down drunk and roaring with laughter as they reminisced about Billy biting the head off of a live lobster on a dare at a New Year's Eve party. One of the guys laughed so hard that he tipped his chair backwards and fell into the refrigerator. When Billy saw the damage that the chair caused, he immediately tried to cover it up. After a lapse in good judgment, Billy decided to paint the refrigerator to disguise the deep scratch in the door. Half tanked, he ran around the apartment and Lord knows where it came from but he reappeared holding a can of paint and a paintbrush. He proceeded to paint the refrigerator a putrid shade of lime green! Paint went everywhere and dripped like rain on the kitchen floor. The more they drank, the louder they got, and one guy grabbed the paintbrush and was about to paint the walls!

Just then Dee Dee came home from the long shift at work, her legs throbbing from standing in heels all night, and all she longed to do was change, relax, and have Billy rub her feet. Instead, she walked in on a party and a hideous, lime green refrigerator. Dee Dee saw red. With a finger pointed towards the door and in a voice that meant business, she screamed, "OUT!" and sobered Billy up in an instant. It was the last straw for Dee Dee – she was exhausted and not at all amused at the sight of her husband and his friends out of control and her neatly kept apartment trashed.

"But Dee, I was just trying to camouflage a scratch!" Billy said.

"I don't want to hear it, Bill. Get out and take all of them with you!" Dee Dee shot back to him.

Billy wasn't moving fast enough and a frustrated Dee Dee had a meltdown. She took off her shoes and threw them at Billy, aiming at his head. Reluctantly, Billy and his friends left, and Dee Dee slammed and locked the door behind him. Billy wasn't used to this because usually Dee Dee would just join in on the fun. I think it was the stress of not knowing how her husband was going to make a living and the fact that he had no urgency to do so infuriated her. Somehow, behind that locked door she felt relieved, even though she faced the momentous task of cleanup.

Billy pleaded for forgiveness and offered to help her, but she just wanted solitude and the chance to calm down. Billy's friends took him to the Forest Inn, a local tavern, to console him. Billy was truly distraught. His head was down on the bar and he was sulking. "I really fucked up this time," he said.

Just then Mikey Jones slapped him on the back. "What's wrong Billy? Who died?" he asked. "I never seen you like this."

"Mikey," Billy slurred, "Dee Dee actually threw me out tonight. What am I gonna do now? I'm broke and I don't even have a place to sleep!"

"I'm going to Atlantic City tomorrow," Mikey said. "Why don't you come with me?"

"And do what?!" Billy muttered.

"Sell Ginsu knives on the boardwalk. You'll make a ton of money!" Mikey said convincingly.

"What's a Ginsu?" Billy said, with a puzzled look on his face.

"Don't worry about it..." Mikey waved Billy off. "I'll hook you up with Ruby Morris and he will teach you how to pitch."

"Pitch? Pitch what? Is this about baseball?" Billy asked innocently.

"No Billy – sales. If it was good enough for Ed McMahon, Charles Bronson, Jack Klugman, and Robert Redford, it's good enough for you," Mikey said, "Who knows where this will take you, and what do you have to lose anyway?"

Billy thought about it and got excited. He wanted a chance to be in the limelight and make Dee Dee proud of him. Mikey told Billy the story about how Ed McMahon became a pitchman and sold vegetable slicers on the boardwalk to pay his way through college. He made five hundred dollars a week off of the Morris Metric Slicer and learned the ropes through Ruby and Archie Morris.

Billy jumped off the bar stool and said, "I'll be right back Mikey – don't leave buddy – wait for me!" Billy staggered toward the door and convinced one of his buddies to drive him home. Once there, he decided to sneak in through the basement window so he wouldn't have to have a confrontation with Dee Dee. The window was locked, so he wrapped his jacket around his fist and punched out the glass. He crawled in through the shattered glass and grabbed the first thing that he saw – an old tattered duffel bag and some soiled clothes in the laundry basket. Like a child running away from home, he crawled back out through the window with the duffel bag over his shoulder and into the waiting car. Billy burst into the Forest Inn's door and shouted, "Come on Mikey, I'm ready. Let's leave now!"

Everyone looked at Billy and Mikey said in shock, "Billy, you're bleeding! What the hell happened? Did you get into a fight?!"

Billy looked down at his shirt that was splattered with blood, and lifted it up to show cuts made by the broken glass of the window. He reached over the bar, grabbed a bar rag, put it under his shirt and said, "Let's go!"

Mikey looked at him with surprise and said, "Man, I wasn't serious! I was just talking – I don't want to be responsible for breaking up your marriage."

Now it was Billy's turn to be surprised. "What's wrong, Mikey? Is this all BS? I feel good about this. I'm begging you man, I need a BREAK."

"But Billy," Mikey pleaded, "Dee Dee is going to kill me."

"Do you want me to get down on my hands and knees?" Billy said.

Reluctantly, Mikey said, "What the hell."

"Don't worry, I'm gonna be the best pitchman on that boardwalk, you wait and see." Billy said excitedly. They left that very night.

Recently, I received word Mikey had passed while working in Columbus, Ohio. Another unfortunate casualty of the pitchman lifestyle.

While Billy went off to the Atlantic City boardwalk to learn his trade and seek his fortune, I headed to Cincinnati, OH to stay with my brother. My brother Lu, and his wife Barbara, purchased an old farmhouse and they asked me to help with renovation. I found solace laying and pointing brick, a skill I had acquired years ago at the Connelly trade school in Pittsburgh. My father encouraged me to go there because I wasn't interested in academics and how right he was! Working with my hands, remodeling this home was my only salvation. When I finished working for the day, physically exhausted, I would go to the local tavern and drink until I was numb. This went on for years and it was a sad existence, but I just couldn't get past being betrayed by my own brother. I even took a blacksmithing course and earned my farrier's license since my brother kept horses on the grounds. Learning something new kept my mind occupied instead of wallowing in self-pity. After five years, with the house completed, I decided to face my fears and move back home. My mother was quite elderly and weak, and I wanted to spend more time with her, my children, and grandchildren. My nephew owned an apartment building in Crafton, Pa and I moved in with my sister Faye and my niece Jan. It was a way to start fresh here and I began doing brick work just like I had done in Cincinnati from '85-'90.

By now, my sons had their own young families, and I enjoyed spending time with them. But something was missing. My internal struggle left me incapable of having any lasting relationship, and my experience being married put me through hell. It was just easier to pick a girl up for the night or fall back on old lovers for comfort and sex. Money has been no problem when I was at the height of my career with my trucking business. Fancy cars, clothes, and vacations - you name it, I had it all. What goes up must come down though, and down I fell from the top of life!

My contribution to the household was minimal. Faye's son Bobby owned the apartment we lived in Crafton, PA. What money I did make laying bricks was used for my own enjoyment. My enjoyment was the "chase" and I loved the conquest. Maybe I didn't drive the Mark V Lincolns or wear the designer clothes, like I had in the late 70s and early 80s, but I still had "the charm."

Remembering back to the good old days, I wonder how good they really were. I judged success by the amount of money I made but I was never able to commit to any one woman. When a woman would whisper, "I love you" I would respond, "I don't know what love is." Looking back, I realize I did know what love was, I just didn't know how to express it.

My son Randy and his girlfriend Lisa insisted that I meet a friend of Lisa's. They said she was different, a lovely girl that was kind and hard working. I agreed to meet her. It was Lisa's birthday and we went to a local restaurant for drinks and dinner. Little did I know that that innocent meeting would change my life forever. I have never been a man of words. I don't express myself that way, but I can tell you that when I looked into Kathy's green eyes, it was love at first sight. She was so easy to talk to and didn't seem at all concerned about what I did or how much money I made. She was used to taking care of herself, standing on her own two feet, and that made her so different from the beautiful but needy, high maintenance women I usually attracted. We seemed to connect on all levels – we liked country music, we both had a strong work ethic, and of course there was a strong physical attraction. Somewhere along the way, I realized all of my past relationships were based purely on lust not love, and I discovered I finally did know what love was. Kathy was understanding, supportive, generous, and giving, besides being beautiful. She provided me with love not only from herself but also from her two daughters as well, who welcomed me into their family.

Kathy and I moved in together and I began to heal. In this woman's arms, I felt safe. She convinced me that I could do anything. I knew I had it all, and I wanted to do the right thing. Here was a good girl with morals, but my fear of commitment still held me back. I had been a bachelor for many years, a confirmed one too, just ask anyone that I have dated! It was Christmas and I wanted to give my love a special gift but I just couldn't come up with anything and time was running out. The idea just came to me that I would ask her to marry me, and when the time came the words were effortless. I knew I was doing the right thing. Little did I know she would give me the ultimate gift – our love is lasting, stronger than ever and things only get better year after year.

In SeaWorld with Kathy, Billy, Elizabeth, Deborah, and Little Billy

Kathy and me

Bobby Paul

Billy with Cris Morris

Billy on Patches
Bottom: Randy, Gary, Mike, Jan, with neighbors

Chapter 11

Horse Incident

Going through the photographs in my suitcase, I happened to pull out a picture of Billy atop a horse. I was watching all the kids ride horses one afternoon. Billy was on a grey Morgan gelding horse, while another boy was on a Pinto pony. Morgan horses are normally very gentle and this one certainly was. Morgans usually don't have very sharp withers and unless the saddle girth is really tight, it'll often slip sideways when the horse shies from something. This day, although the horse was four years old and usually ignored things being swept by the wind, a large pheasant flew up in front of the horse. He spooked and sidestepped quickly. Billy, like the horse, was startled too, and when his horse went one way, Billy went the other and fell. Luckily, the ground right there was pretty soft and as I rushed over to him and saw he was all right, he got up, brushed himself off and went over to the horse. Billy remounted and insisted on continuing to ride. This was one of the first examples I had of his ability to "get back on the horse" when the time called for it.

Chapter 12

Dee Dee

I was trying to chronologically organize some pictures and this lovely photo of Dee Dee fell out of the stack. The two women who were most influential in Billy's life were his grandmother and his mother. He loved women and he respected them. I recall stopping by the high school to watch Billy's football practice and I stuck around afterwards to give him a ride home. I'm glad I did because Billy seemed burdened by something and needed to talk. When Billy told me about this sad, young girl he would see on the sidelines, I could tell (I knew) he had deep feelings for her.

Dee Dee was a cheerleader at Sto Rox High School in McKees Rocks and since Billy was a football player there, the friendship blossomed. I remember Billy confided in me about Dee Dee because she already had a boyfriend, and Billy was concerned about this relationship. "Dad, she isn't being treated like she should. To me, she is a princess, and I wish I could ride in on a white horse, scoop her up, and take her away with me."

In high school, Billy was dedicated to football. He always stayed late to work out or run. His senior year, he was the MVP of the Sto-Rox team. He used to talk to Dee Dee in the alley behind the school. She was emptying the trash and he was running. They talked every day in the alley. She was being bullied by her boyfriend and hadn't told anyone, not even her family. She confided in Billy and he took care of that. She was grateful and fell in love with him.

It wasn't long after that before the two became "high school sweethearts" and were inseparable. Dee Dee came from a big Italian family and with them Billy felt right at home. The two dated exclusively all through high school and Dee Dee became part of our family too. Even when Billy went away to WVU, and Dee Dee stayed behind to attend Pitt, she would take the bus to Morgantown so they could spend weekends together.

Other girls came and went through Billy's life but he always seemed to come back to Dee Dee. She gave him the sense of family – something Billy clearly wanted. The relationship evolved into something more because it was almost expected by both families that there would be a wedding eventually. After leaving college, Billy and Dee Dee shared an apartment together. Dee Dee was Billy's security blanket, so I wasn't surprised when he decided to marry her. To this day, I stay close to Dee Dee and I recently asked her how Billy proposed. She thought about it and said, "I never remembered him asking. It just happened." Billy and Dee Dee got married in February of 1984, after having dated on and off for nine years.

I can still see the couple at the altar of Mother of Sorrows Church (St. John of God) in McKees Rocks. Billy was terrified and noticeably ill, still under the effects of the bachelor party the night before. His black hair was full and eighties big – and he now had the trademark black beard and mustache. As he spoke his vows, you could barely hear him. He hadn't grown into his voice and he certainly didn't know how to project yet! This was the real Billy before he became an actor to play the part of Billy Mays the pitchman. Next to him was his cousin, Dean, who seemed to be with Billy through all the important times in his life. They were partners in crime, almost like brothers.

There came the angelic Dee Dee, her petite frame enveloped in the big, white wedding dress. She was looking up at Billy with all of the love and hope every young bride has. As I watch that scene back in my head, I remember wishing that they would have a long, solid marriage full of love and respect, with lots of children. The wedding was a traditional Catholic ceremony, and the reception was an elaborate affair at the Churchill County Club in Churchill, PA – provided by Dee Dee's Aunt Louise.

The next day, the kids borrowed my Lincoln and drove down to FL to honeymoon. Billy and Dee Dee really gave this marriage a go! Even though my business declined and Billy was out of a job, they were perfectly happy in their little apartment. In those days, I remember Dee Dee was quite the sales-person. She sold shoes in a posh boutique at Station Square on the South Side and she was very successful at it. Billy would drive her to work and pick her up after 8 hours or better on her feet. Dee Dee never complained because she was so madly in love with Billy, things like this never mattered to her. Billy would cook and try to keep up with the house while Dee Dee was working, but the wheels in his head were already spinning.

Billy thought his Nuna Alma made the best Italian wedding soup in the world! He begged her to teach him how to make it and she was so flattered that she acquiesced. Billy practiced and practiced and he and Dee Dee ate wedding soup every night for a week because he was determined to perfect Nunna's recipe and make it his own. I really think Billy's career began at Station Square, when he convinced a snack shop owner to sell containers of his wedding soup to his hungry customers. How I wished he had patented that recipe and made his first million with the soup!

Even though everyone raved about Billy's recipe, the ingredients were expensive, it was a lot of work, and he wasn't making a profit. Just as things were coming along, while Billy was delivering the first major order, my clumsy son tripped over his own feet and spilled the entire, massive soup pot all over the floor of Station Square! Everyone stopped what they were doing to get a glimpse of the accident, and once it was clear he was okay, everybody had a good laugh about it. I guess Billy didn't laugh about it too much though, since soon after that he decided the soup-making business was too much trouble and gave up on it.

What most people don't know is that when they started working together, Billy and Dee Dee made a hell of a sales team. Billy and Dee Dee would sell anything to make ends meet, and they kept their lives fun and carefree when possible. When Billy's friend suggested he go to Atlantic City to pitch products on the boardwalk, he went along—and the rest is history. Soon after they were married, Dee Dee quit her job and went on the road with Billy. Chris Morris, the owner of National Kitchen products who employed Billy at the time, gave Dee Dee her own booth and she was pitching miscellaneous items: chamois, dusters, or whatever they asked her to sell.

Billy and Dee Dee spent the holiday season of 1985 pitching at a Boscov's in Binghamton, New York. Known as "The Valley of Opportunity," it reminded them a little of Pittsburgh since it was also on a river, too. Dee Dee was pitching whistling key chains by the elevators of the department store while Billy was pitching his beloved WashMatik in another area of the store. It was an unusually hectic day and the couple decided to walk home for lunch to the furnished apartment they shared around the corner, to take a break from the holiday madness. The snow began to fall and Billy put his arm around Dee Dee and pulled her close to keep her warm. Dee Dee recalls, "It was a particularly good lunch," because that was the day their son was conceived! She remembers the Dire Straits song that was playing on the radio –they only had a radio; there was no TV in the apartment, they really couldn't afford it then. They made their own entertainment. When they went home for Christmas, Dee Dee was one month pregnant. She didn't have to make an announcement because her family guessed she was expecting by the look in her eye and how happy she was.

Dee Dee worked on the road all nine months of her pregnancy. The couple had planned on taking time off at the end of August when the baby was due, but the baby had other ideas and came early. Billy was working at the Columbus, Ohio home show when he got the news that his wife was in labor and he made it back for the last two hours of labor - the pushing! When Billy came in, all dressed in scrubs, exhausted, excited, and admittedly scared, he knocked everything down in his wake! Remember, Billy was quite clumsy and in the excitement of the whole situation and becoming a new father, he charged into the room to be by his wife's side. Billy had medical instruments pinging off the floor, the contents of the room falling like dominos, and all you could hear was noise and banging. The labor nurses insisted, "Mr. Mays, if you don't calm down, you will have to leave!" Billy quietly stood in the background and soon William D. Mays III came into this world on August 12th, 1986.

After the birth of her son, Dee Dee longed for a more traditional lifestyle. Billy was back on the road and she was home caring for Little Billy. Dee Dee and her sister Linda were born eighteen months apart and were very close. Linda was Dee Dee's confidant and she would tell her sister that Billy should come back home to Pittsburgh and find a regular job with benefits and be a husband to her. The relationship between Linda and Billy had always been strained. Even in their younger years, Linda and Billy seemed to vie for Dee Dee's attention. If Billy would stay out late with his friends, Linda was the first to notice and plant the seed of doubt in her sister's head. This led to many arguments, and Linda and Billy fought bitterly. It was somewhat fortunate then that Linda met and fell in love with a man from Switzerland and eventually moved to Europe with him. In the meantime, Dee Dee would visit Billy on the road with the baby in tow when she could. Billy continued to work and send money home to support his family. This was a lonely existence for the young mother; she missed her husband and she had a lot of time on her hands to think about it. Linda suggested that Dee Dee and Little Billy should come for a visit and Dee Dee jumped at the chance because she also missed her sister so much. The Swiss Alps were beautiful and the time spent in the peace and solitude there gave her a chance to clear her head. She realized that life on the road was just too hard and was not the way she wanted to raise her son. By now, Little Billy was a toddler and Dee Dee started thinking about the idea of having another baby. She was bitter that she was in Europe by herself, enjoying the beautiful sights but without sharing the experiences with her husband. Right then and there she decided she had to make a change, and she built up the courage to speak her mind.

On the way back from Europe, since Dee Dee and three-year-old Little Billy had a layover at JFK airport in New York City and Billy happened to be working at a nearby home show, they arranged to meet at the airport. Dee Dee caught sight of Billy bounding towards them, carrying a huge teddy bear with a big red bow. Little Billy squirmed out of his mother's arms and ran to his daddy that he missed so much. The reunion was bittersweet, however, because Dee Dee was determined to have a showdown. She loved Billy so much that when she saw him she usually put their problems behind them and just enjoyed being together - but not this time. Billy put his strong arms around his petite wife and enveloped her, but instead of melting into his arms, she stiffened.

"Billy, I can't do this anymore. I want you to be a husband to me. I am so tired of being alone!" Her voice cracked, she was shaking, but the well-rehearsed words came out. "Unless you are willing to stay home and be a husband to me, I can't live like this anymore. I want to have another child, maybe a daughter for us, but not without a father that is there to help raise these children."

Billy was shocked at her words. "Another child is not realistic right now Babe, and you know I'm on to something here but I have to be on the road for a while. Dee, if you can only be patient a little longer I am going to make it. I know it, Dee, I just KNOW it! All I have to do is find the right product and you'll see, things will change for us." Billy said those words with such strong conviction that it threw Dee Dee off a little, but she had heard it all before. She had had enough and without hesitation and without making eye contact, she reached for her wedding ring, took it off, and put it in Billy's hand. The three stood crying in the middle of JFK, not knowing what would happen next. In hindsight, Dee Dee regrets not waiting longer, but it was just too hard and she gave up on their dreams. I'd known her since she was fifteen, and hearing that the family was splitting apart, my heart went out to both of them. It was history repeating itself – too much drive, too much ambition, too much work, and not enough time with the family.

The bug of success had bitten and Billy was making money and sending it home to his family, but the once inseparable couple had no contact. Holidays came and went, but Billy was driven to work and make money rather than celebrate and make memories. Having a son changed the fun loving young man into a responsible father, but he was never home to be a father and husband.

Billy and Dee Dee

Billy's bride and her
five sisters

Billy and Dee Dee
and best man cousin Dean

Left: Billy and his mother Joyce
Below: Me dancing with Dee Dee

Welcoming Little Billy

Christening of Little Billy
at St. Malachy's Church

Billy turns 30

A Mays Family
Christmas.

Little Billy
and me

Mays
family portrait

Chapter 13

WashMatik

I pulled out an old picture of Billy demonstrating the Wash Matik. These were the very early years when money didn't come easily but somehow I think Billy was having fun. "Bucket Billy" got his nickname because of the Wash Matik that was nothing more than a valve and a hose. You used your own bucket to create running water when an outside spigot wasn't available. Veteran pitchmen jealous of Billy's success with the WashMatik would kick his bucket of water over to ruin his demonstration. Billy didn't get upset; he would fill up ten buckets of water. He gained respect from the elder pitchmen when they realized how tenacious he was.

Billy had a few friends that would travel with him and help him set up. He made his name on the Atlantic City boardwalk but there were many long, hard stops along the way. He would work "Super Sales" at malls setting up his Wash Matik in the center aisle along with many other vendors trying to promote impulse buying, and hoping this was the item people couldn't live without. One particular stop was at the mall in Ashtabula, OH right in the heart of Amish country. As Billy set up with high hopes of a big day, all he could see was women in bonnets and long, dark skirts and men with dark hats dressed very simply. He smiled and the people wouldn't make eye contact with him. They kept their gazes down and seemed somewhat cynical about what was going on. Remember this was Amish country where old-fashioned living, hard work, and honesty are a way of life.

As he started his pitch, he could hear snickering from the people passing by. He knew it would be a tough crowd and he had his work cut out for him. NO ONE WAS SELLING ANYTHING! The Amish aren't impressed by bells and whistles, they are a people of practicality. The image of these people reminded him of his German grandma, Nuna, a no-nonsense woman who raised six children without running water in the early days. She was a hard-working farmer's wife and I remember her fretting about the well and whether we were getting enough rain. She remembered the days of carrying water in buckets to the house and the chance of the well going dry.

How could he market the WashMatik to people who didn't buy frivolous gadgets? If we didn't get enough rain, the well would go dry! A light came on in Billy's head and he got the biggest smile on his face! He figured out how to get the Amish to understand his product. What is the most important possession to an Amish farmer? His horse! Not only was this their only form of transportation, but also their horses plowed their fields and lightened their burden. As the crowd milled around, Billy shouted out the question, "How do you wash your horse?" Men and women alike stopped in their tracks and started laughing with puzzled looks on their faces. Once he got the crowd's attention, he knew he had them. Farmers depend on wells in this area and water is precious. You could wash and rinse your horse with 2 buckets of water. Billy shouted at the young unshaven men, "Don't you want your horse and buggy clean for your best girl? Don't you want to take good care of the animal that takes good care of you?"

Magically he became like an Evangelical preacher in a church full of parishioners – they hung on his every word. While the other vendors stared in amazement, the money started rolling in. As Billy sold and told his funny anecdotes about farming and horses, his friends were collecting the money hand over fist. They netted over $5,000 that afternoon.

Billy could sell anything but this was Billy at his best – pitching something he believed in and figuring out how to win his audience. Sometimes I think it wasn't about the money; it was about winning and helping people.

Billy's rise to fame was almost synchronistic. One of the biggest things to happen in his industry occurred in 1984, when the FCC deregulated and allowed companies to start airing half hour commercials to sell their products. "Infomercials" as they would quickly be nicknamed, were a whole new direction and approach for sales, and Billy was right there at the beginning with the promotion of the WashMatik. He went on to represent many products and was the spokesperson for OxiClean, but he also made Tom Motosko a millionaire with his invention, the Awesome Auger.

Some of the other, well-known products that Billy also pitched were:

- Orange Glo: "It cleans and protects in one easy step"
- KaBoom NeverScrub: "Does your toilet have hard-water stains or a ring of rust that keeps coming back?"
- Mighty Mendit: "It happens! You rip, tear, and never have time to repair."
- Mighty Putty: "The easy way to fix, fill, and seal fast and make it last"
- OxiClean: "Get on the ball, and you'll never have to pour or measure detergent again."
- Quick Chop: "The fastest, easiest, safest way to chop, mince, or dice any vegetable guaranteed."
- Simoniz Fix-It: "Uh Oh, that'll leave a mark. Stop the scratches!"
- Tool Band-It: "Tired of fumbling with your tools, or wasting time trying to find them? Do you ever wish you had an extra hand?"
- What Odor?: "Are you tired of using sprays that only mask odors?"
- Greater Plater: "What would happen if you combined a cheese grater with a plate? You'd have a plate that grates!"

And there were many, many more than that…

Hulk Hogan and Billy were in Las Vegas when Hulk asked him what he was getting for being the spokesperson for OxiClean. Billy said one million – Hulk laughed and said he should have been getting six or seven million. But like I said, it wasn't just about the money. Billy was a natural born salesman but he had to believe in the product to sell it.

On the road to Detroit with
Little Billy in 1986

Wash-Matik
demonstration

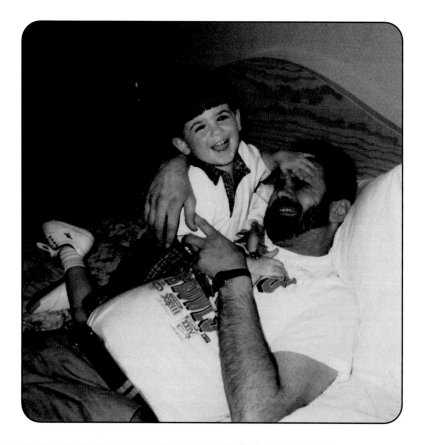

Billy and little Billy with Terry "Hulk Hogan" Bollea

Chapter 14
Billy and Jamie

A lot of these photos are thrown in that suitcase in a haphazard kind of way, and stuck to the back of Dee Dee's picture was a picture of Billy and Jamie. Dee Dee had met Jamie when she was 15 and she was on the road selling with her parents. Billy called Dee Dee and told her that he started seeing Jamie. She was about 20 at the time. Billy said, "That is where my life is going to be." Dee Dee had trouble letting her only son go to visit with Jamie and Billy but Jamie was good to Little Billy and Dee Dee gradually became okay with it. The relationship, however, wouldn't work out.

It was a few days before Christmas and I was just putting the final touches on the tree that I had cut down the day before. Shopping done, gifts wrapped, house ready for Billy's arrival. I was like a child waiting for Santa to come! The bowls were washed and ready for the endless supply of shrimp Billy would devour and my homemade hummus and pita. I tried to set examples of healthy eating for Billy. Eating on the run all those years made Billy change his diet, as he got older. We spent many hours talking on the phone about healthy foods, supplements, and vitamins. Billy loved the water and swimming was his exercise. Because of his hip he was limited, but the water kept him pain free.

Kathy would always take Christmas week off but we were both working just as hard around the house as if we were at work, getting ready for Billy's arrival. I woke up that Christmas Eve morning and did my checklist one last time. Before I knew it, the door swung open wide and Billy bounded into the house. It was as though Santa had arrived – gifts, hugs, laughter; those were the days I will cherish forever

Behind Billy was a voluptuous, sun-kissed blonde. She made an entrance like a model on the catwalk. Billy introduced us to Jamie. As I reached to shake her hand, she walked towards me, and a cloud of Chanel fragrance wafted through the room. Jamie was wearing a full-length blush mink coat that Billy had bought her for Christmas. After all, it was winter in Pittsburgh, and Billy wanted her to be warm.

I remember Kathy staring at her with her mouth wide open. We thought maybe she was a movie star but we weren't sure. After all, Kathy and I are busy working and don't have much time to keep up with Hollywood gossip.

Life was starting to become good for Billy. He looked happy and healthy with Jamie. The two worked the Orange County flea market, the biggest flea market I have ever seen, as well as home shows, auto shows, and state fairs. Working noon to 10 p.m. seven days a week was nothing to them. They worked hard and played hard at night. Their competitiveness was never to be mistaken for envy but rather camaraderie. This was the code of brotherhood among pitchmen. Billy and Jamie would get together after a long day with brother pitchmen and relax and unwind while bragging about who sold the most, who made the most money, who was loudest, who grabbed the brass ring. Jamie and Billy did this together for twelve years before he got his big break with Oxi-Clean.

Whenever he was in Pittsburgh during the holidays, Billy would always stay at the Sheraton in Station Square for a week. He rented a huge suite so he could entertain friends and family during the holidays. Party time! Plenty of Jack Daniels, food and wine, and good times! Billy spared no expense to ensure that everyone had a good time. Those who went and didn't enjoy themselves were the few that were jealous of his success. What a shame that was. He only wanted to share with those he cared about. Billy was Billy and he never forgot where he came from. He never put on airs – just Billy Mays from McKees Rocks, PA.

When he'd first get back into town, he'd always give me a call to meet up and get a bite. "Hey Dad! Jeet?"

"No, d'ju?" I'd say. He still spoke with his Pittsburgh accent, his Pittsburghese grammar, and he proudly never changed or corrected it.

"You wanna meet on the Sahside, or Dahntahn?"

After the holidays, Jamie and Billy returned to the apartment they shared. Billy loved the beach and always wanted to live by the water. When I visited my son, we experienced California together. I remember just Billy and me stopping for dinner at a local seafood restaurant right on the beach. Lobster, Dungeness crabs and cold beer – what could be better? There was a beautiful sunset over the water that night and happy memories for me.

Enter Max Appel…

I was looking for a picture I remembered taking while on that vacation to California, but when I fumbled around in the suitcase I found an article from a magazine that I had stapled together. It was about being in the right place at the right time, and how having an empathic nature can change your life. The article was how Billy met Max Appel, the founder of Orange Glo and eventually Oxi Clean. As I read the words, I remember Billy telling me the story. He was working at a home show, Bucket Billy with his WashMatik. Billy was getting a little competition for the crowd from Max Appel, who was selling Orange Glo wood cleaner right next to him. Billy always told me that you have to sell yourself as well as the product to win over the crowd. Both men were enthusiastically engaging the mob of people that had gathered around them when Max fell silent. Engrossed in what he was doing, Billy didn't even notice that Max's microphone had cut out until he saw him jiggling the thing out of the corner of his eye. When he had closed the sales at hand, he walked over to Appel, who was trying to yell in the loud, crowded venue, which wasn't working too well. They often bumped into each other as they worked a lot of the same shows, so Billy offered Max the use of his spare microphone. Billy felt fortunate that he was able to learn his craft of pitching and break into the business, so he never passed up the opportunity to help someone out. Due to this act of kindness, Max and Billy became friends but were still rivals when they were working at a show. In 1996, Appel called Billy to see if he was interested in pitching Orange Glo on TV. Billy liked the product, and he used it. So he agreed. In time, Billy helped produce, write, and pitch Orange Glo infomercials, and a year later OxiClean came along. By this time, Home Shopping Network executives had noticed Billy.

Billy's break to Home Shopping Network meant moving to Florida. He and Jamie rented an apartment right on the ocean. Billy knew Jamie would miss CA and he did his best to recreate the life they had had there. The hours at HSN were grueling and Jamie was home with nothing to do. She was in a new environment and home by herself most of the time. Billy, on the other hand, was busy and doing well financially. He decided to buy a house in Clearwater right up the road from the beachfront apartment. Billy felt the larger space was better for Jamie and the house had a beautiful pool. They also bought a couple of English bulldogs to keep her company, Winston and Ellie Mae.

As they say, "The apple doesn't fall far from the tree," and my workaholic ways were passed to my son. The calls from Billy would come as early as 4:30 a.m. Billy wasn't sleeping in those days, and he knew I was up. The stress of working and trying to keep Jamie entertained was taking its toll on Billy and their relationship. I recall him saying he knew Jamie was unhappy when she would drink Vodka for breakfast. It wasn't long after that they decided to split, and although Billy gave the house to Jamie, she eventually moved back to California.

Jamie was suing Billy for palimony. They were together for seven years, and lawyers worked out an agreement where Jamie got the house in Florida and a lump sum. Dee Dee was shocked at what she walked away with, but Billy was always generous to her, too. Ultimately, Jamie sold the house and moved back to California. It was rumored that she donated her money and proceeds from the home to Scientology.

Dee Dee and Billy were very close and told each other everything: who they were dating, or about their son. Before he married Deborah, they talked about getting back together. Billy was home in Pittsburgh for a week and they spent a lot of time together with their families. Billy was very tired and looked wiped out. Four cell phones rang constantly and calls from all over the country – all over the world came in. As much as she loved him, she didn't want to sit around while the phones went off and he was on the phone all day. She got a preview of what her life would be like, and she didn't want that. Dee Dee was confident at the time. She had a good job and was taking care of herself, and she was content to raise Little Billy. Billy discussed his plans to marry Deborah, and Deb and Billy actually came to Dee Dee's house and asked her to come to their wedding. She took the high road for the sake of the relationship between Deb and her son. Dee Dee wanted to set an example for her son, Billy III.

Dee Dee and Billy stayed close even after his marriage to Deborah. Deborah told Dee Dee shortly after the wedding that she didn't want kids, that the relationship was hard enough. There came a time that Deborah thought Dee Dee was too involved with Billy and their marriage.

Billy, Little Billy, and Jamie

Chapter 15

Home Shopping Network

I remember the time I went to visit Billy on the set of Home Shopping Network. We went back to the prop room where the Oxi Clean fish tank was filled with water. As Billy pushed the fish tank to the stage, water sloshed everywhere! He was always a little bit clumsy, but I think it was the beginning of the hip problem that made him walk that way. I would sit in the studio and watch Billy perform as he demonstrated Oxi Clean. Sometimes we would spend the whole day there to tape one sixty-second commercial. Finally, Billy and I would watch the monitor with excitement knowing the more he sold the more he made since he made a percentage of everything that was sold. He was under an exclusive contract with Oxi Clean. When Oxi Clean was sold to Arm & Hammer for millions of dollars, Billy didn't get a penny out of the deal. Turn about is not fair play, since Billy was responsible for making Oxi Clean a household name. I asked Billy about the sale on one of our phone calls, and he said, "you win some and you lose some. The company dangled a carrot and I fell for it."

Billy didn't play the stock market. His talent as the Pitchman was his private stock. There were other perks of being well known on TV. Billy appeared as a television personality on ESPN and ABC's college football coverage. Having been a passionate football player himself, these opportunities to analyze and critique the game from this perspective gave Billy endless satisfaction and enjoyment. I think those sports guys liked having him on there, because of his personality and because he knew what he was talking about.

I happened to pick up a copy of the *Washington Post* I'd saved where they referred to Billy as a, "full-volume pitchman, amped up like a candidate for a tranquilizer gun take-down." The negative press didn't stop Billy - in fact it became a challenge for him. Billy was basically a humble, shy type of guy. He considered himself a sensitive person. He believed in balance and would say to me, "Dad, as long as there's good and bad, it evens itself out."

There will never be another Elvis and there will never be another Billy Mays, although there are plenty of imitators.

Even though he didn't reap the rewards of the sale of Oxi Clean, HSN is where he met Deborah. He became enamored of her and it didn't take long before things got serious between Deborah and Billy. Billy sent Kathy and me on a Caribbean cruise and it was agreed that we would spend a few days in Tampa with him afterwards. As we departed from the ship, Billy met us. He seemed nervous and excited when he told us about the plans he had made for that evening. "Dad, we are going out to dinner, and I want you and Kathy to meet my girlfriend!" That evening, as we were driving to dinner in the Rolls Royce, I remember how preoccupied Billy was. I'll never forget the look on his face when, upon our introduction, I shook her hand and said, "I'm happy to meet you, Debbie."

"Dad" he shot back, "Her name is Deborah! Deborah!" I knew he was serious when he looked into her beautiful eyes and repeated her name again. Now, many years later, I call her Deb, but the memory of that meeting always makes me smile.

Billy and his many
products

Billy on set
with his
mother Joyce

Chapter 16

Deborah

Billy and Deborah were introduced by a mutual friend in the business. She caught the attention of every man around her, especially Billy. Deborah was a buyer for Home Shopping Network. Their paths crossed and he was smitten. He would tell me, "Dad, I can sell millions of dollars of products and always have the right pitch, but I can't find the words to talk to this girl. I am tongue tied around her." I would laugh and remember the shy, little Billy as a kid. His voice was his weapon but he was at a loss for words around his Deborah. Most of our phone calls around that time were all about Deborah.

I could hear Billy's insecurities coming out, as he would describe her. "Dad, she is beautiful, young, and a class act. I don't know how to act around her."

I said, "Just be yourself, Son. True love is when you can be yourself around someone and they love you just the way you are." To which his constant reply would be, "Thanks Dad! I love you." And so he found his way into her heart.

I can only imagine how my son eventually proposed to Deborah. Was it in the Range Rover or Rolls Royce? Was it on the beach? What a wedding! Two hundred and fifty people gathered together in a posh hotel in Tampa. Out of this union came the joy of his life, Elizabeth. When Billy spoke of Elizabeth you could hear his voice soften over the phone and he spoke of her with love. Little did I know that Elizabeth would be the one next to Billy when he died. I want to live long enough to make my visits with my granddaughter moments of joy.

Christmas portrait of Billy and Deborah

Chapter 17

Billy and Deborah's Wedding

I remember this morning was a cold, bleak February day. I thought, "when's spring gonna get here?!" I settled into my favorite chair with a steaming mug of coffee and put another log on the fire. From my house atop the city of Pittsburgh, I can see all the way down to where the 3 rivers meet. If I look to my left, I can see the Ohio River and just a few miles down the Ohio you come to McKees Rocks, PA – hometown to Billy and our family. As I thought about the family, it reminded me that I wanted to go get the DVDs I had made from old movies of the kids out of the little suitcase and watch them. I smiled as I gave a thank you to Billy for my beautiful 46-inch state-of-the-art TV. Randomly, I just put in a DVD and it was of Billy and Deborah's rehearsal dinner.

Look at my son, Billy, the only one there with shorts on. Billy loved to be different. When Billy married Deborah, he rented a huge condo in Disney World, Florida. We were all there, including my brother Lu and his wife Barb from Cincinnati. Billy knew that my sister Ruth wouldn't be comfortable in her wheelchair on a plane, due to her Multiple Sclerosis, but Billy made sure that she and her husband Leo would be at the wedding. So generous Billy arranged to have her, her husband Leo, and their car driven to D.C., then taken by train down to Florida! Billy loved his family and wanted us all there. We had a wonderful time before, during, and after Billy's wedding.

As I watched the rehearsal, I could see the love in Billy's eyes for Deborah, and I knew it was genuine. The next day, at the ceremony, I watched as Billy said the words "till we're parted by death." He always said this was the happiest day of his life, and I believed him.

At the wedding, many of the guests said a few words about the day and gave congratulations to the newlyweds. I paused the DVD and rewound it so I could hear Deborah's twin, Dan, again. Her brother was now telling his twin he could take off the boxing gloves because she was in good hands and would be protected by Billy. Dan thanked Deborah for giving him a brother (Billy), and then I heard it. Dan said, "I am looking forward to spending a couple of years together with you." Billy quickly responded, "Forever!"

I wonder if being a twin, Dan had a premonition of what was to come? The word "forever" kept coming out of the well-wishers and I fought back the tears. It was painful for me to watch, but I had to get past the pain to spend some time enjoying seeing my son. It's hard to believe that Billy almost called off the wedding after viewing this tape.

Both brothers, Randy and Gary, received numerous calls days before the wedding from a very anxious Billy. Nearly in tears and hyperventilating, he begged brother Randy to come to Florida and offered to send a private jet to fly him to Tampa. Randy said, "You have to take care of this yourself, big brother. Take my advice and run like hell!"

Being a minister himself, Randy didn't approve with the religious beliefs of Deborah and her family. They put too much stock in the word of the so-called spiritual guide. Randy said she has a spirit of divination. Not knowing what that meant, I looked it up. It means to follow the words of someone who is using props instead of following the word of God. Her props are the cards that Billy talked about.

Not getting the answer he wanted from Randy, Billy jumped in his Bentley, drove up to Plant City, FL, and showed up at his brother Gary's doorstep. "I saw the desperation in his eyes," Gary told me.

"What's wrong? Did something happen to Mom or Dad?" asked Gary.

"No Gary," Billy said. "I don't think I can go through with the wedding. Fifty thousand. Fifty thousand," he kept repeating like a mantra.

"Fifty thousand what?" Gary asked.

"Fifty thousand to buy my way out of this wedding. What should I do Bro?" Billy pleaded.

"Billy, you just drove up here in a hundred and fifty thousand dollar car! What is fifty thousand for your happiness? That doesn't make sense. What's wrong with you? I always thought you should have insisted on a prenup," Gary said.

"I can't," Billy said. "I am afraid of what she would say."

"Well Brother, that's a red flag right there. Besides, I would never be with a woman that treats me like crap. Remember I was with you the first time you ever went to her house – I knew she was after you for your money." Gary admitted.

With a dejected look on his face, Billy said, "I'm holding out for Deborah to change – I have a fifty-fifty chance that this will work."

Who knows? Maybe it was just Billy getting cold feet? This will always be a mystery to me, one of those things I'll never know the answer to, or will be able to ask him about.

As the song "The Wind Beneath My Wings" started to play, Billy scanned the room for his mom. She beamed as they danced and Joyce always said, "That's my boy." Billy would do anything for her and he even gave her the car she drives today.

Billy was the center of attention as always. He was a John Travolta wannabe – off came his shoes and then the jacket. The DJ played "YMCA" and Billy donned a full Indian headdress. Billy danced by himself to "Kung Fu Fighting" just like he used to when he and Dean went to the clubs back home. Billy was asked to be on "Dancing With the Stars" but had to renege because of his hip. I'm sure he would've been a contender for the mirror ball trophy!

Joyce's husband, Don, sang lovingly to the newlyweds as they danced to the song, "Once in a Lifetime." People would pay for the evening entertainment – it was like watching a Lou Rawls show in Vegas. The reception went on until after midnight and no one wanted it to end. Little did we know, Billy and Deborah would only have five years together.

Billy and his mother Joyce

A father and son
thumbs up!

Don, Me, Deborah, Billy, Little Billy, Joyce, and Kathy

Chapter 18

Odessa House

Billy's pride and joy was the Odessa, Fl home and the *House Trends* magazine jogged my memory of it when I came across it in the suitcase. My mind took me back to this palatial paradise located on Journey's End and the many visits my wife and I enjoyed there. This home, Billy's dream home, was where we shared so many good times as a family. Every inch of the home was geared towards entertaining and comfort. Billy and Deborah had the home built with this in mind and spared no expense to design and furnish the perfect retreat.

Kathy and I felt like we checked into a five-star hotel when we walked into the guest suite. Each guest bedroom had its own en suite bathroom and separate terrace for private space. The master bathroom was a spa – rainforest shower, vessel sinks, and a roomy Jacuzzi tub with heated towel racks. It made you never want to leave! With 9,000 square ft. of living space, a pool, and a lanai complete with an outdoor kitchen, every amenity was under one roof. I was so proud of my son! Billy was raised in a simple apartment in the projects of McKees Rocks and it was hard to fathom how far he had come.

Billy liked to cook, and I think that rubbed off from me. When the boys were growing up, I always cooked Sunday dinner for them. That was important to me to give them that stability, but I wasn't married at the time so I would go through magazines, find a recipe I thought they would like, go the grocery store, and make their dinner. Maybe that is why Billy liked to cook for me when I came to visit?

We would jump into the Range Rover or the Bentley, and drive to Publix to pick up steaks or veal chops, Billy's favorite things to grill. You can imagine the attention that we got when we went shopping, but Billy never felt infringed upon. In fact, he loved being recognized – he ate it up! I remember how patiently he would talk to the employees and customers at Publix. People would come up to us and say, "Aren't you a celebrity? You look like that Billy Mays that shouts on TV!" Then Billy would go into his spiel, "Billy Mays here!" and give them a big "thumbs up." Billy always stopped to talk or sign autographs and he loved being in the spotlight. He never forgot where he came from, so he always made time for his fans.

From the grocery store, we would go to the health food store. Billy would spend hundreds of dollars on vitamins, supplements, and fish oil – anything that would give him the stamina to keep up with his busy lifestyle. We both believe in the health benefits of drinking fresh wheatgrass, and I remember Billy insisted on buying a wheatgrass juicer for me. We shared a love for good food and also practiced moderation; we often tried the Master Cleanse and eating healthy, vegetarian diets. I also grow my own sprouts, and we would shop for tools for sprouting.

When we returned home, the fun began! Little Elizabeth, Billy's daughter, would run around playing with her little toy horses, and Billy and I would unpack the groceries and cook for the girls. Billy would say, "Go pick out a bottle of wine for us, Dad." I have never seen such a collection of wines – it was like being in a liquor store after hours! We would enjoy a glass of wine and grill a delicious dinner. After dinner, we would take a walk down to the lake and watch the fish jump. Even though my son Billy was so busy, he always took time off to spend time with us when we visited.

As you enter the home through the massive front door, one of the first things you notice is the breathtaking Swarovski crystal chandelier in the foyer. I asked Billy what kind of ladder he used to clean it because believe it or not, he not only pitched cleaning products - he actually liked to clean! With all of his usual enthusiasm he said, "Watch this, Dad!" as he flipped a switch and the chandelier dropped from the ceiling like a scene from "Phantom of the Opera." "This is how you clean a chandelier," Billy laughed. For a brief second in that moment, I got a glimpse of Billy around age 4, curled up in his bed, sound asleep with all of the lights on. He always needed a lot of lights on, especially at bedtime, because even as a grown man Billy was afraid of the dark. I know the reason why, but it is something I will never share and will take with me to my grave, next to Billy.

Pittsburghers are very proud of the rich history of their professional sports teams, and Billy was no exception. In a room overlooking the lake, behind his lavish, well-stocked bar, the focal point of the entire room were, large display cases filled with Pittsburgh sports memorabilia. Signed balls, jerseys, pennants, you name it – he had it. Billy saw this as an investment, and if it were something that attracted his eye, he'd spend as much money as necessary to add that prize to his impressive collection.

The house had a theater complete with a sound system and a huge screen where I would get lost watching *Planet Earth* and nature shows. Billy did voiceovers there for his commercials so the sound system was professionally installed. In fact, speakers were hidden in the walls of the whole house, even in the planters! Billy loved music and he liked to dance and sing to relax. Music carried all the way to the pool and the gazebo on the lake since speakers were located every 15 feet. Two coconuts in the palm tree by the pool vibrated with music.

At first, there were no trees, absolutely no landscaping around the home, as it was new construction. Billy then had 30 foot palm trees brought in to make it an island paradise. The mature palms looked like they had been growing there for years.

Imagine my shock on one of our regular phone calls, that Deborah had convinced him to put their magnificent house up for sale and relocate to South Carolina. The obvious beauty of this home made me wonder what would possess my son to ever want to leave this utopia. I should have asked him more questions... My biggest question would have been, "Why would you move from your dream house – the house where you always said, 'they'll have to take me FEET FIRST out of here!'" Billy and Deborah built the Odessa home together with all of their strict specifications. I could hear the sadness in his voice and I tried to get him to open up to me.

"Dad, it's a long story and I doubt you would even believe it, but I have lived apart from my son as he was growing up and I'm not about to live apart from my daughter." I knew this was serious – but Billy was so much in love with Deborah I couldn't imagine that their marriage was in jeopardy. Billy told me that Deborah had an intuitive friend that had a great influence on her and her family. In fact, it was this friend that chose Odessa as the location for the Florida home. Because of Hurricane Katrina, Deb's family friend convinced her that FL wasn't a safe area and she used a deck of cards to choose an area for where they should move. I thought this was one of Billy's jokes – he was quite the comedian. But as I laughed, I could tell he was serious. The card she chose was a bird and she equated that to South Carolina's state bird. We talked longer than usual because my son sounded defeated and it scared me. When we finally hung up, I immediately called my ex-wife, Joyce, Billy's mother. She had also spoken with Billy that day and he told his mom if he had to start over and build another house it would break him. We were both very concerned – we knew this wasn't right, but Billy was a grown man with proven business sense, so who were we to tell him what to do?

Deborah's family friend considered herself a self-proclaimed prophet, and during one of the sessions she would have with Billy and Deborah, Billy told me she would speak in many tongues. She gave them all note tablets to write down the messages she would receive. Any decision that had to be made would be made together, and then she'd draw cards and she would decide what it meant and they would follow her suggestions. Billy didn't believe in that stuff. He went along with it because he loved Deborah.

When Billy's mother Joyce, her brother, and his wife went down to Florida, the day Billy passed away, Mary (Deborah's mom), and the family friend were standing in the kitchen. The first words out of their mouths were, "Poor Deborah has to get a job now. Billy didn't have a will or any insurance." I thought that that was an odd thing to be saying to a grieving mother, whose son had died the night before. More odd was the absence of a will since he traveled so much, and especially because family meant so much to him and he always wanted to make sure everyone was taken care of properly.

It appeared that something came over Billy – he seemed to hypnotically go along with all of this because of the strong ties between a father and his daughter. He hated to go on business trips and leave his precious Elizabeth behind. She would wait outside and jump up and down when her daddy would finally come home. I never had a daughter and I never felt I missed out on anything until I saw the look on Billy's face when she was in his arms with her tiny arms wrapped tightly around his neck. She was his world and he would move heaven and earth to keep her there. When he finally purchased the property in Greenville, South Carolina, he bought an extra lot as an insurance policy. If anything happened to the marriage, he intended to build a house right next door so he could always be in Elizabeth's life. Billy was in his late forties when his daughter was born, and he was a devoted father. His life was his work and his family was his life.

Foyer and chandelier   Stone fireplace

Gameroom

Billy's office

Kitchen and
breakfast bar

Family Room

Pool

Corvette

Rolls-Royce

Billy and me, with the Bentley

The home in South Carolina
Billy never saw completed

Chapter 19

Journey's End

Billy told me about Deborah's trip to Pittsburgh her conversation with the wife of a family member, and the repercussions of that trip. Deborah and the relative's wife were talking about their husband's participation in running the home, particularly the finances. The young wife felt the husband should be in charge, which immediately rubbed Deborah the wrong way since in their clan, the women made the decisions. I couldn't believe what Billy was telling me. "Dad, as soon as we returned from Pittsburgh, Deborah withdrew all of the money out of our checking account and filed for divorce! She got a divorce attorney, which cost ten thousand dollars, and this is a big mess." Now he was telling me Deborah wanted a divorce! I didn't want to pry, but Billy wanted to talk. I couldn't believe my ears. How could a successful man be telling these stories? If Billy's good friend from Florida hadn't validated this to me later, I never would have believed it. Billy said that Deborah refused to have sex unless it was for the procreation of children. I laughed and said, "Billy, you better stop taking those pain pills – they are making you crazy!"

He said, "Dad, I only take what I am supposed to and have more to tell you." I remember my wife walking past me as I was talking to Billy. She said my mouth was hanging open in disbelief and she kept asking me, "What's wrong? Is everything okay?" I had to take a deep breath and compose myself. Then Billy told me about the bathroom scenario. Billy's bathroom was like a car wash – huge! It had rainforest showerheads with different levels and pressures. It's where he relaxed and pleasured himself since his wife had no interest in sex. Deborah walked in at an inopportune moment and was appalled at what she witnessed. He started to tell me about magazines and I was feeling embarrassed.

I said, "Billy, why don't you come back to Pittsburgh and you and I can talk this over."

"Dad, I can't run away from this situation. I have to tell someone." I never had this conversation with him again.

Obviously, Billy wasn't happy in the marriage and knew it was in jeopardy. Billy and Deborah sought out a marriage counselor. Part of the arrangement was that Billy shouldn't have so much contact with his ex-wife Dee Dee. To break this off would break Billy's heart because he still had very strong feelings for Dee Dee. It was her that he called when he brought Deborah and Elizabeth home from the hospital. Billy said, "Dee, I swear to God, I missed out on raising Little Billy and no matter what happens I am going to raise this little girl." Billy felt trapped, and his only confidant was Dee Dee. He wasn't about to give up his relationship with the one woman he truly felt he could talk to.

I tried to convince him that his daughter was his daughter for the rest of his life. I think at this point, Billy had mixed feelings about his marriage to Deborah because of the influence other people around her had on his life. He didn't want his life to be dictated by a woman reading cards to direct their lives, but he loved Elizabeth so much that he was willing to put blinders on and go on with life. Billy was even contemplating starting a radio talk show that he could produce from his home so he could stay close to Elizabeth. These are my opinions from our conversations; I could read between the lines.

A trusted friend of Billy's (who refers to himself as Billy's other brother) confirmed that Deborah insisted that Billy beg for forgiveness for satisfying himself – not only to her, but in front of Deborah's mother and the self-proclaimed prophet who advised the family! I would have never thought something like this was possible if he hadn't told me, but now I could truly believe it for myself. I can only imagine my son's humiliation. The manipulation began when they met and Deborah convincingly portrayed herself as a woman in love with Billy, drawn to him sexually and emotionally. She wanted to marry him and relocated when he had doubts. He bought a big ring and went after her. After the marriage, the domination began, and eventually he was forced to sell the house of his dreams. Finally, Billy faced the humiliation of having to explain details of his marriage that should be kept private between a husband and a wife.

I remember Billy telling me how he changed Elizabeth's diapers and wanted to be involved in raising her because he regretted not being at home with Billy III. I can relate to this because I wasn't around to help raise my boys. I thought providing for them financially was what I was supposed to do. Emotionally I wasn't there, and it was the ruination of my marriage.

I didn't want this to happen to Billy again, so I supported his decision. Whatever he decided to do, I respected it. Due to the economy, the magnificent Odessa house was slow to sell. Deborah, being a very meticulous woman, felt if they were living in the house with a young child it wouldn't be in pristine condition for showing. She encouraged Billy to rent a condo in Tampa until the house was sold.

Rent, a mortgage, funding the building of another home, not to mention a third hip operation looming over his head, were all weighing on his mind. What if this operation wasn't successful? His doctors warned Billy that he could only have one more operation. I am sure he was frightened by the bleak possibility that he could be confined to a wheelchair. All of this was taking a toll on Billy. It seemed to me the more money you make, the more money you need. Billy was traveling more and more – working on the Pitchmen series – working on a deal with Taco Bell.

Becoming the spokesperson for Taco Bell was the pinnacle of Billy's career. I remember how we joked about our appetites and how we could eat all the tacos we wanted. I said to Billy, "I don't like tacos so much."

Billy said, "Doesn't matter Dad. They will taste like money!" and he laughed.

As Billy reached this certain level of success I thought, "Isn't this enough? How much more do you need?" I had hoped my son was taking time to enjoy life, to enjoy what he already had. Billy always picked me up at the airport in his Bentley and it made me feel like a celebrity too. But what was the cost?

LIEUTENANT
WM. B. MAYS
ROBINSON TWP. POLICE

Chapter 20
Heart Disease Doesn't Make Headlines

I think the dark side of success is when you become too busy trying to keep ahead of yourself and every one around you happy. Billy couldn't take time to take care of himself. He was too busy trying to make more money. My son followed his heart to fame, but he didn't take care of his own heart. My father, Wm. Benton Mays, died at the age of 68, while on duty as a police officer, of a massive heart attack. My son Gary, one year younger than Billy to the day, is on his second pacemaker in twelve years. I myself had a pacemaker put in two years ago. My brother Teddy also had a pacemaker and died from complications of a stroke. I am concerned about Billy's son, Billy III, and pray that he will always take care to look after his heart. Now I wish I would have insisted that Billy do something a few years ago when the first signs appeared. We were having lunch together and I noticed Billy wincing and tapping his chest. I asked, "What's wrong, Billy?!" His answer was that he must have eaten too fast and lately he felt his heart skip a beat. In my ignorance, I am sad to say I didn't respond to what I now know as a warning sign. Now, I am educated to the facts of congenital heart disease. Today, because of modern technology, I am alive and so is my son, Gary. I call it, "The curse of the Mays men." Whenever I hear people say that cocaine was the cause of Billy's death, it infuriates me! I found out recently that the reason Deborah had an independent coroner's report performed was because in the event Billy died of an overdose, she would not receive royalties from his commercials. Billy didn't need to use drugs to get high. He was high on his ego and his success, and it came out in his commercials.

I forgot over the years that both Gary and Billy were born with heart murmurs. Gary had his first heart attack in his 30s, while driving a truck through West Virginia. He slumped over the wheel and blacked out. The EMTs on the scene wanted to transport him to a local teaching hospital, but Gary insisted on going to Pittsburgh to his own doctor. He had been treated there since the age of 12 for his heart and they knew his history.

In 1996, with no warning whatsoever, Gary rolled his truck over. At this time he was diagnosed with a slow pace to his heart and had the first pacemaker implanted. Gary remains healthy but has blood work performed every 3-4 months as a precaution. I suppose that is why Billy was so protective of Gary. Billy orchestrated Gary's move to FL and helped financially when needed. It was Billy who helped Gary get through the tragic death of his 27-year-old son just two months prior to his own passing.

It was a rainy day in April when my son, Randy, called with news about Gary Jr. At the time of his call, he said, "Dad, Gary is dead!" I felt dizzy and couldn't believe the words; my son dead at the age of forty-nine? I thought his heart issue had been resolved with a pacemaker and I couldn't make sense of this.

I came back to the conversation and I said, "Was it his heart?"

Randy explained, "No Dad, little Gary never had heart problems." Little Gary was twenty-seven years old and healthy and I was confused. Randy is a patient, kind-hearted man and he slowly explained to me that it was my grandson who died. Poor Gary, he was dead at such a young age with no explanation; yet another Mays tragedy. The news traveled fast through the family. That afternoon I was compelled to drive to his house, trying to get some answers. I knew he was having problems with his ex girlfriend regarding their son, Juliano. If my memory serves me, the child was just a toddler at this time. Gary was having financial problems as well and was about to lose his car. Why didn't he ask me for help? As a boy (about age twelve) he worked for me for extra cash, and he was an excellent worker. As he got older, we talked at length about staying healthy and I remember I bought him a juicer because he seemed so interested in taking care of himself. I'll never know what happened to that boy, but he is always in my prayers.

Billy came in for the funeral and I recall how emotional he was to see his nephew lying in a casket. Billy was close with all the kids, but only when I overheard his conversation with his ex-wife, Dee Dee, did I fully understand why. Billy put his hands on Dee Dee's shoulders and said, "That could have been our son in there" and he broke down in tears. Billy III and his girlfriend Whitney were victims of an arson case in their apartment in Florida. A disgruntled tenant set fire to the building upon being evicted. The building was burned down to the ground and Billy and Whitney were lucky to escape with their lives! All of their possessions were destroyed, all of the music Billy III had written, and all of his musical instruments. Billy III said they moved so recently that he didn't have time to purchase renter's insurance, so all was lost, but fortunately they survived.

My son, Billy, looked so upset at the funeral I was concerned about his health then. Even Dee Dee mentioned to her son, Billy III that his father looked awful, like a limp rag. Billy III reassured his mother that it was just his long hours at work and he was working too hard. Dee Dee wasn't satisfied with that and she walked up to Billy and told him, "You look awful."

He hugged her and said, "It's my hip, Dee. I am taking the pills prescribed for me but I am in so much pain". That was the last time Dee Dee saw Billy alive.

Gary spent a lot of time with Billy during the period after his son's death. When I asked Gary about his relationship with Deborah, he stopped for a few minutes to ponder over my question. The answer I didn't want to hear came out of his clenched teeth. He said, "Dad, there WAS no relationship between Deborah and myself. She didn't even want to come over to visit me and she was upset when Billy and I got together." These two brothers were very close given the fact that they were only one year apart. Gary told me things of Billy's marriage in confidence that I would never divulge to protect my grandchildren. I am not even sure my daughter-in-law will permit a future relationship with Elizabeth once this book comes out?

I do know that Billy loved Elizabeth and Billy III more than anything on earth. He told me about his purchase of the lot next to his house in South Carolina. "Dad," he said, "If the marriage doesn't work out, I will build a home right next door and always be there for Elizabeth." Billy not being sure things would work out was a big departure from "forever" that Billy said in his vows.

Reluctantly agreeing to move from his beloved home in Odessa was a traumatic ordeal for Billy. He cried whenever we spoke of this, and I kept my thoughts to myself. Billy's mother Joyce said that Billy once confided to her, "If I have to build another house it will break me," and ultimately it did. It didn't break him financially, but I now believe the stress of the Odessa home contributed to his death. Ironically, the name of the address is "Journey's End." Back then I would tell Billy, "Things have a way of working out. Just be as good a father as you can be." I wonder to this day what would've happened to that marriage down the road. Billy was tiring of the control Deborah was placing on him.

As I heard Kathy coming in the door from work, I realized I had spent the whole afternoon reminiscing. I glanced at my watch, Billy's watch that Deborah gave me a few months after Billy died. The watch jolted my memory about the time Deborah surprised Billy with a Rolex she purchased for him from her cousin. The price of the watch was $40,000 and she was happy that her cousin would get the commission on it. When she presented the watch to Billy, he promptly returned it. He told me it was much too ostentatious and I gathered he didn't want her to spend money so frivolously.

Celebrating Little Billy's graduation
from Full Sail

The condo Billy
lived in at the time
of his death

Chapter 21

Humanitarian Tribute to Billy

Upon my recent return to Pittsburgh from Florida, I was eager to watch the CD Sully had given me. Anthony Sullivan was Billy's partner and together they starred in the Pitchmen series on the Discovery Channel. Billy invited me to come onto an episode of the Pitchmen and feature an invention that I'd come up with thirty years earlier: a chaise lounge that turns while you are sunbathing. I came up with this invention years ago when sun tanning was popular. Billy named it "Turn Don't Burn" because the chair had a motor that gradually moved you one rotation every minute so you wouldn't get too much sun in one area. Billy encouraged me to patent the chair because he thought we could market it to hotels or cruise ships. The big day came and the "infamous" chair was filmed around Billy's pool.

There was my invention flanked by beautiful models in bikinis hired to demonstrate the features of my chair. That was the first time I was ever on television. The last time was at Billy's funeral. Shortly after that was filmed, Billy died and I lost my passion to pursue promoting my invention.

My reason for visiting Florida was to spend some time with "Little Billy" as we call him. Billy III and I went to the Strawberry Festival together just like Billy and I used to do. Oh how my son Billy loved to walk the grounds, stopping to shake people's hands, as they followed him as though he were the Pied Piper. They begged for an autograph or a picture with him. I remember a young boy sitting in his wheelchair in the crowd around Billy. Billy spotted the boy and said to me, "Dad, take a picture with me and the boy over there." The boy put his hands out and Billy gave him a great big hug as I snapped the picture. Tears came into my eyes and I knew Billy still retained his compassion and humanitarian, empathic nature. He later told me he wanted to give back to people less fortunate than himself.

Billy talked about starting up a foundation for children. He wasn't sure what he wanted to do, but he was working on it. Billy's friend Kevin Farley said Billy helped him cover thousands of dollars of unpaid bills. Their son, Ryan, has Tourette's syndrome and insurance wouldn't cover all of the medical expenses. Kevin fondly remembers when Billy asked him to come to a home show in Balitmore. "Billy knew I always wanted to fulfill my Irish heritage. When we got to Baltimore he had a surprise for me. He'd made arrangements to go to the Cat's Eye, an Irish pub located at Fells Points, a waterfront community dating back to the 1700s. That night I felt I was really in Ireland as we danced and sang with the locals at the bar. This is what made Billy so special – he was always trying to make other people happy."

Kevin and Billy had been friends since junior high school and Kevin was in both of Billy's weddings. After Billy passed away, Kevin was so devastated he couldn't go to work for two weeks. He designed a tattoo in honor of his best friend Billy. Kevin still has the last voicemail Billy left on his answering machine the night he died – apologizing for not being able to attend Ryan's graduation because of his surgery. He never got a chance to talk to his buddy again.

At Christmastime, Billy would give cash to his brother Randy to help people in McKees Rocks. The only stipulation was that he remain anonymous. It was up to Randy to distribute the money as he saw fit. Randy used the money to buy carloads of Christmas gifts, fixed cars, paid mortgages, rent, gas, light, and cable bills. Randy estimates the amount of money to be at least fifty thousand dollars, and he thinks that's a conservative estimate.

Billy also had a hundred and eighty thousand dollars earmarked for his brother Randy, an ordained minister, to purchase the St. Mark's church complex in the McKees Rocks bottoms. But to use Billy's words, there was a new sheriff in town, after he married Deborah. She didn't share his philanthropic ways and disagreed with backing Randy's ministry and the church project. Even though the church idea fell through, Billy continued to give money to Randy to help those that needed it in McKees Rocks, unbeknownst to Deborah. Billy was very generous with his money, but Deborah, I assume, had other intentions for it.

There is also the story Billy told me about doing commercials for I-CAN insurance. A couple came up to him, and the husband had recently lost his job. They bought insurance through I-CAN just before the husband was diagnosed with cancer. They told Billy if it weren't for him telling them to get insurance, they wouldn't have been covered.

Billy said, "It was the most humbling experience of my life, Dad. Even if I had to wear the damn blazer on TV." It was the first time he was "out of uniform" on TV. I remember many times when his generosity changed people's lives. Billy was the godfather for his friend Mike Sappe's child. When the boy tragically died from a heart defect, Mike had no money for funeral arrangements. Billy jumped on a plane and was the first person on the scene to help. He quietly paid for the funeral, while he continued to console his friend. It wasn't the last time he took care of financial hardships. When his friend and fellow pitchman Bobby Paul passed away, Billy insisted on paying for that funeral too.

That evening when I was alone with my grandson I was sharing the memories that the Strawberry Festival evoked. I hope that Billy III remembered all the summer vacations spent with his father. Billy even invited his son to bring a buddy so he wouldn't be alone. When it was time to select a college, Billy was all for his son attending Full Sail College to study music. When he graduated, Little Billy moved in with Billy and helped him with voiceovers in the studio at home. Just as I watched my son on the Jay Leno show many times, I get the feeling that someday I will be watching my grandson Billy there as well.

I hope that Billy III will bring pleasure to people with his music and make a difference like his father. The time spent with my grandson was priceless, and a comment he made touched me. He told me my mannerisms and just being with me reminded him of his father.

At an industry awards ceremony where Billy was nominated for an achievement award, even though he wasn't sure if he'd win or not, he was really nervous. When the time came for comedian Paul Rodriguez to announce the winner, Billy was off in the restroom and they couldn't get him to come up to accept his award. As boisterous as he appeared in front of television cameras in the studio, or a small group of strangers on the boardwalk, the idea of standing up in front of his peers petrified him. When they finally found him and pulled him up on stage, and handed him the beautiful piece of crystal that was the award, clumsy Billy dropped it and it chipped!

Every September, the Electronic Retailing Association presents its "ERA Awards" for the best infomercials of the year. After he passed away, the best male presenter award was given posthumously to Billy for his work on the Omni Dual Saw infomercial. Also, Pittsburgh Mayor Luke Ravenstahl bestowed the honor of designating September 20, 2009 "Billy Mays Day" in Pittsburgh, recognizing what he had accomplished in his life. I will always cherish that certificate, a reminder of all he was and did in his brief time here:

MVP award winning linebacker on the Sto-Rox Football Team

Salesman for Mays Corporation before moving to Atlantic City, NJ, where he learned his new sales technique from elder Pitchmen and traveled for twelve years across the country selling various products

Billy's television career started in 1996 on Home Shopping Network where his voice became famous and he pitched OxiClean and OrangeGlo

Founder of Mays Promotions

In 2009 starred in and produced the Pitchmen *series on the Discovery Channel*

Received an award for best Infomercial of the Year in 2002 and was posthumously presented a Lifetime Achievement Award by the sales industry

Honored at the Emmys for his work in the television industry

Always proudly promoted his beloved hometown of McKees Rocks and the Pittsburgh area

My dream is that with the possible success of this book, to have a bronze statue of Billy placed somewhere in McKees Rocks. Billy would've liked that, because he liked things big. For all his boisterousness and the image people had of him, Billy wanted people to know the real Billy Mays – not just a yell and sell. That he was a very generous, humble guy and that he worked hard. He loved making people laugh and he had a heart of gold. I hope I've been able to relate a little of that by telling my story, and he'll be remembered for all of the things he did in the brief time he was here.

Thumbs up!

Congress of the United States

House of Representatives

Whereas, The life and times of the renowned television pitchman Billy Mays will be commemorated on September 20, 2009, as Billy Mays Day is celebrated at a memorial concert at Sto-Rox High School, Pennsylvania; and

Whereas, Born on July 20, 1958, in McKees Rocks, Pennsylvania, William "Billy" D. Mays, Jr. graduated from Sto-Rox High School in 1976 after receiving the M.V.P. award in football as a linebacker on the school's team. Billy embarked in his tremendously successful career in product promotion on the Atlantic City Boardwalk in 1989. Through hard work and perseverance, he eventually distinguished himself as our nation's most recognizable and beloved television pitchman and has been recognized for his outstanding achievements in the industry; and

Whereas, His proud family and the entire community mourns the loss of Billy Mays whose vibrant personality and indomitable character captivated each and every one he touched. His remarkable journey of success epitomizes the American spirit and stands as a testament to his enduring legacy.

Now Therefore, As Representative of the 14th Congressional District of Pennsylvania, I join with the Sto-Rox community in recognizing and commending and exceptional accomplishments of Billy Mays and extend heartfelt condolences upon his passing.

Mike Doyle
Member of Congress

Commonwealth of Pennsylvania

The House of Representatives

Citation

Whereas, The House of Representatives of Pennsylvania takes great pride in recognizing those citizens who, through their exceptional achievements, bring a notable measure of pride to themselves, their communities and this Commonwealth; and

Whereas, William D. Mays, Jr., is being honored posthumously at the 2009 Emmy Awards on September 20, 2009, and also being awarded a posthumous Lifetime Achievement Award in Las Vegas through the television industry; and

Whereas, The son of William D. Mays, Sr., and Joyce Hoffman Palm, Mr. Mays was born in McKees Rocks on July 20, 1958. His family included his wife, Deborah Wolley Mays, two children, William D. Mays III and Elizabeth, and two brothers, Gary and Randy. Mr. Mays was a 1976 graduate of Sto-Rox High School, where he received the Most Valuable Player Award in football as a linebacker. He began his professional career in Atlantic City in 1989 and signed a contract with the Home Shopping Network in 1996, becoming a television direct-response salesperson. The sponsor of more than one hundred fifty products, Mr. Mays was a guest star on **The Tonight Show with Jay Leno**, **Late Night with Conan O'Brien** and the **Rachel Ray Show** . Founder of Mays Promotions, Inc., he received an award for Best Infomercial of the Year for OxiClean in 2002 and was featured in a documentary series on the Discovery Channel entitled **PitchMen**.

Now therefore, the House of Representatives of the Commonwealth of Pennsylvania pays tribute to the late William D. Mays, Jr., on his richly deserved recognition; affirmatively states that he stands as a role model worthy of emulation;

And directs that a copy of this citation, sponsored by the Honorable Nick Kotik on September 20, 2009, be transmitted to the family of William D. Mays, Jr.

Nick Kotik, Sponsor

Keith R. McCall, Speaker of the House

Attest:

Anthony Frank Barbush, Chief Clerk of the House

CITY OF PITTSBURGH

OFFICE OF THE MAYOR

A Proclamation

By virtue of the authority vested in me as Mayor of the City of Pittsburgh,
I do hereby issue this proclamation honoring

WILLIAM D. "BILLY" MAYS, JR.
September 20, 2009

WHEREAS, William D. "Billy" Mays, Jr. was born in McKees Rocks, PA. He graduated Sto-Rox High School where he received the M.V.P. Award as linebacker on Sto-Rox Football Team. He left West Virginia University and worked for his father's hazardous waste company before moving to Atlantic City, New Jersey; and

WHEREAS, Billy began his career as a salesman on the Atlantic City boardwalk. It was there that he picked up his sales technique from older pitchmen. For the next 12 years he traveled cross-country selling various items; and

WHEREAS, Billy's friendly manner and booming voice caught the attention of national television and in 1996 he began his television career pitching OxiClean, Orange Glo and other products for the Home Shopping Network. Over the next several years Billy sponsored 150 different products; and

WHEREAS, Billy's pitch was so unique he soon became known as the nation's celebrity "pitchman." He was the founder of Mays Promotions and in April, 2009 the Discovery Channel began airing "Pitchman, a Documentary," featuring Billy Mays, Jr.; and

WHEREAS, in 2002 Billy Mays, Jr. received an award for the best infomercial of the Year and in September 2009 he was posthumously presented a Lifetime Achievement Award by the sales industry. He will be honored at the Emmys for his work in the television industry.

NOW THEREFORE BE IT RESOLVED that I, Luke Ravenstahl, as Mayor of the City of Pittsburgh, do recognize William D. "Billy" Mays, Jr. as America's most famous pitchman and deeply appreciate his continued promotion of his hometown of McKees Rocks and the Pittsburgh area. I do hereby declare September 20, 2009, "Pitchman Billy Mays, Jr. Day" here in our most livable City of Pittsburgh.

Luke Ravenstahl
LUKE RAVENSTAHL
Mayor

Billy and best friend Kevin Farley

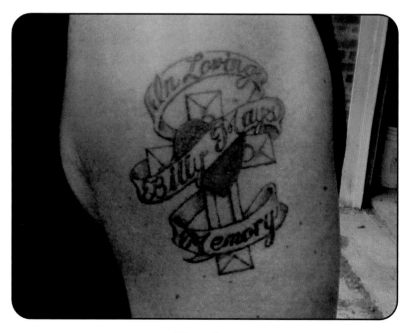

Kevin's tattoo in memory of Billy

Semi-Pro with the Sto-Rox Rangers
Top row:
Chuck Bucek (general manager) Butch Patterson (head coach)
Bottom row:
Bud Hackimen (defensive captain) Billy Mays (offensive captain)

One of
Billy's talk show
appearances

My "Turn Don't
Burn" chair

Acknowledgements

Many thanks to Karen and Jim Dunn, the proprietors of the Foggy Mountain Lodge in Stahlstown, Pennsylvania for providing us with a most beautiful setting. We spent many hours at their cozy lodge putting this book together, and they always went out of their way to make us comfortable.

About Marc E. Virostek

Marc Virostek is a Pittsburgh native. He became interested in local history and the characters and stories of the Pittsburgh region at an early age, after a gradeschool field trip to the Fort Pitt Museum. In addition to writing & editing, he is an avid artist, photographer, and librarian. He is currently working to finish a photographic book project highlighting the many locations and forms of the Great Seal of the City of Pittsburgh throughout the city.

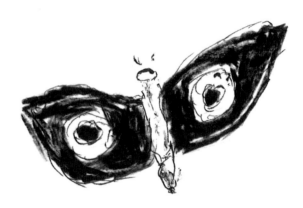

The Silver Spotted Skipper

Bottom: Drawn by the author, from memory

Silver Spotted Skipper

Before you set this book down, I wanted to relate a strange experience I've had several times in the last couple of years. What I first took as a complete coincidence has become a clear sign to me that I was meant to write this recollection of Billy, not only for myself and for others, but for Billy too. Of course, you can be the judge of what it all means, but for me it's undeniable.

I was in Greentree, PA on July 3, 2010, a little over a year after Billy died, unloading wood from the back of my pick-up and a butterfly landed on the wood and stayed there until I finished and then it flew away. The very next day, I was at Mike's house, where we've been celebrating the 4th of July for years with a holiday picnic, and the same exact butterfly was hovering around a table outside where Billy had liked to sit. It flew inside and landed on the table. This got my attention, but I wrote it off as coincidence.

Right after I finished the book and was on my way to the publisher's, one of those butterflies landed on my windshield at a stoplight. I remember being unsure about this whole thing because I knew parts of the book would probably upset some family members, especially my daughter-in-law. I didn't want to jeopardize my relationship with my granddaughter Elizabeth either. I didn't write this book out of malice, and I remember thinking, "What should I put in or take out?" When the light turned green, and that butterfly was still on the windshield, hanging on for dear life, it seemed to be saying it was okay to move forward with the book just as it was.

The latest and last time this strange appearance of a butterfly occurred was a few weeks ago. I was sitting in my open garage with my helper, Sam, and we were sitting there and having a beer after work and that same familiar butterfly flew in. I stood up and jokingly said to Sam, "Look Sam! There's Billy," and held out my hand, never expecting it to land. But it did, and it stayed on my finger for a good minute! Sam and I were both speechless – all he could say afterward was "Wow! What was that?!" While the appearance of the butterflies the first two or three times could be considered a random coincidence, I really feel this last experience confirmed they were all signs from Billy.

I haven't seen a butterfly since, but I did come across an article in a magazine confirming my suspicion. The article is about a mother devastated over the loss of her son. Her sister, the boy's aunt, prayed for a sign to tell her the young man was okay and to bring some peace to her grieving sister. The sign was a butterfly – just like mine! And just like me, she goes on to believe that the repeated visits couldn't be explained any other way but as a sign.

I looked in a book and found out the butterfly is a Silver Spotted Skipper. How appropriate, as it's described as having "rapid, darting flight." I have to smile at that. Yep, that's Billy all right!

WA

Made in the USA
Las Vegas, NV
11 November 2023

80650877R00100